Souvenirs of a Blown World

BY GREGORY MCDONALD

Running Scared (1964)
Fletch (1974)
Confess, Fletch (1976)
Flynn (1977)
Fletch's Fortune (1978)
Love Among the Mashed Potatoes apa *Dear M.E.* (1978)
Who Took Toby Rinaldi? (US title) / *Snatched* (UK title) (1978)
The Buck Passes Flynn (1981)
Fletch and the Widow Bradley (1981)
Fletch's Moxie (1982)
Fletch and the Man Who (1983)
Flynn's In (1984)
Carioca Fletch (1984)
Safekeeping (1985)
Fletch Won (1985)
Fletch, Too (1986)
A World Too Wide (1987)
Exits and Entrances (1988)
Merely Players (1988)
The Brave (1991)
Son of Fletch (1993)
Fletch Reflected (1994)
Skylar (1995)
Skylar in Yankeeland (1997)
Flynn's World (1999 as e-book; 2003 on paper)

NONFICTION

The Education of Gregory Mcdonald (1985)

Souvenirs of a Blown World

Sketches from the Sixties
Writings about America: 1966–1973

Gregory Mcdonald

Seven Stories Press
New York ✦ Toronto ✦ London ✦ Melbourne

Seven Stories Press
140 Watts Street
New York, NY 10013
www.sevenstories.com

In Canada: Publishers Group Canada, 559 College Street, Suite 402, Toronto, ON M6G 1A9

In the UK: Turnaround Publisher Services Ltd., Unit 3, Olympia Trading Estate, Coburg Road, Wood Green, London N22 6TZ

In Australia: Palgrave Macmillan, 15–19 Claremont Street, South Yarra, VIC 3141

College professors may order examination copies of Seven Stories Press titles for a free six-month trial period. To order, visit http://www.sevenstories.com/textbook or send a fax on school letterhead to (212) 226-1411.

Book design by Jon Gilbert

Library of Congress Cataloging-in-Publication Data

Mcdonald, Gregory, 1937-2008.
 Souvenirs of a blown world : sketches from the sixties : writings about America : 1966-1973 / Gregory Mcdonald. -- 1st Seven Stories Press ed.
     p. cm.
 "Originally published as The education of Gregory Mcdonald by Warner Books, April 1985"--T.p. verso.
 ISBN 978-1-58322-866-1 (pbk.)
  1. United States--Civilization--1945- 2. Popular culture--United States--History--20th century. 3. Mcdonald, Gregory, 1937-2008. 4. United States--Description and travel. I. Mcdonald, Gregory, 1937-2008. Education of Gregory Mcdonald. II. Title.
 E169.12.M2575 2008
 973.92--dc22
                                        2008043103
Printed in the USA.

9 8 7 6 5 4 3 2 1

Contents

In memory of I.T.E.M.

Also dedicated to Ian Forman, Fortunato "Nye" Rosa, Eugene Brackley, Gilbert Friedberg, Steven Hansen, and John Driscoll.

Introduction

It was not a time of great men, but of great people.

The 1960s were an era, an era as distinct as the 1850s or the 1920s, a veritable roiling sea among the landlocked years, a colorful, wind-whipped lagoon with monsters in its deep, a time to remember, a time to forget, with its own denim fashions and drug deliriums, of mass hopes and popular despairs, raucous music and anguished silences. America was twenty again, confronted with deceptive prosperity and an indecent poverty, a righteous peace and an immoral war. We had a conscience, and confusion. Sights changed. Sounds changed. Feelings changed. Our perceptions changed. A new base line, as uncertain as all others, was established through which all personalities and institutions had to pass to find a means of survival.

The decade began with the riots at the Newport Jazz Festival in 1960, when beery, crew-cut youths in khaki Bermuda shorts suddenly rioted, for no reason then known, and got themselves arrested. It began with the new Civil Rights Movement. It also began with the election of John F. Kennedy in 1960 to the presidency of the United States. Whatever else was said about him, John Kennedy made the whole world believe it was moral and fun to be young and healthy. His assassination in November 1963, somehow made the young and healthy instantly feel like members of a counterculture. The world was handed back to the same old uglies, tired politicians, entrenched institutions, reactive rather than initiative ways of doing business. To paraphrase Abbie Hoffman, just "being" was subversive. Having seen a hopeful sunrise, we were not yet ready for the dark. As Phil Ochs put it, from the moment of John Kennedy's assassination, the whole history of the country, day by day, became blacker and blacker, more and more insane.

As a reporter of this era, I believe a few observations in particular need be explicitly made.

As the Industrial Revolution profoundly and permanently changed the way in which humans related to nature, to each other, and to themselves, so also does the Technological Revolution.

During the 1960s, more than half the population of the United States was under thirty years of age. With alarming rapidity, technology was diminishing the need for this huge population in the workplace. Whereas historically a person's work, on the farm or in a factory, usually could be counted on to support himself and a few others, a family, the technology factor developing in the 1960s indicated that the work product of a single person could support sixty people, by now, hundreds of people. Contrary to the previous strong American work ethic, social systems were contrived to keep people off the labor market. Deliberately, youth was prolonged, by compulsory education to the age of sixteen, by the newly common experience of college and then university education, by the Selective Service System, by the Peace Corps. Unemployment insurance and the welfare systems were expanded to include as much as a quarter of our population. Social Security was liberalized to encourage early retirement among an ever-increasing sector of American population.

For the first time, we had the vision, the reality, of a population sitting isolated in electronic boxes, a diminishing number of us being genuinely productive.

Underlying the 1960s was our initial reaction to the new technology.

The car was no longer a luxury but a necessity, especially in the new American cities such as Los Angeles and Phoenix, essential to our making a living, an external self, a steel suit of clothes. Jet airplane travel, plentiful and cheap, further shrank concepts of time and space for an increasing percentage of our population. One out of three American families during this era moved house every year. The human intellectual leverage granted by the computer was no longer extraordinary but had become a familiar adjunct of everyday life. No longer were we citizens, workers or students. We were whirring numbers seen through a little window on a computer tabulator. Our personas and our privacy had been lost in a stack of punchcards. There could be nothing romantic or glamorous about a war, however far away, which we could witness daily on our television screens in closeup color. Gone forever was the Churchill-Hemingway-John Wayne romanticizing of war as a macho adventure. Nightly scenes of bloodied teenagers writhing in agony on jungle grass that day in far-away places dispelled that myth forever. For much of the population, pastoral nature, even the visible working of human muscles in a factory, had been replaced by electronic boxes, urban glass, steel, cement, wires, ourselves seen flickering on television screens. Our need to have a physical sense of ourselves and each other became a demand for openness and honesty with ourselves and each other. As the need for physical work diminished, the demand for physical exercise increased. As traditional ways of relating to each other became dominated by electronics, the demands for psychotherapy and synthetic grouping in political, religious, support and cult organizations grew. The contraceptive pill and intrauterine devices discouraged the nest-building tendencies in our sexual relations. Our increasing electronic isolation intensified our need for each other physically and emotionally. The touch of formality among us, necessary to protect family and future as economic and emotional concepts, was replaced by the demand for immediate honesty in our relations with each other.

Evidences were beginning to appear that work, mental and physical, was being replaced to an ever greater degree by activity generally nonessential to the basic survival of the individual. Instead of a necessary product being the result of one's activities, more and more the activity itself was seen to be the goal, the product.

And of course the thermonuclear holocaust was not just a phenomenal possibility. It had been a historic reality since 1945; a mind-staggering reality to which little adjustment had been made in the generation between 1945 and 1960.

I combine quotes from two of my father's broadcasts, August 6 and 7, 1945, the moment of the first use of the atomic bomb on Hiroshima, Japan:

> It is sometimes extremely difficult to grasp the full significance of a fact. We hear a statement, for example, or we witness an event, and we understand it according to the knowledge we already possess. Sometimes many years must pass, and great volumes of wisdom added to our original source, before we comprehend the full content, before we are struck with the whole impact of that earlier disclosure. We learn, for example, that a certain constellation is so many light-years distant from the earth, but not until we have actually figured out the length of a light-year does the shocking truth dawn upon us that the brilliant vibration which we are now watching is coming from a planetary body which may have ceased to exist a million years ago.
>
> It is in some such dimension as this that we must regard the news which came from the White House late this morning. In a statement issued by President Truman, the United States War Department is now using an atomic bomb against Japan.
>
> An atomic bomb is one in which destruction is wrought by atomic power—the power concealed in an atom of matter. The vision of science, the ultimate goal of decades of research has been achieved.
>
> The very basic and elemental power of the material universe has now been made subject to the will of Man. The force from which the very sun in the heaven draws its physical dynamic has now been harnessed and reduced to the servitude to the human race.

It is a day unrivaled in history when this news can be told. And it should be a day of prayer, that this new servant may not turn against his master; that this new secret of inconceivable might may never be used for evil purposes . . .

For atomic power can, indeed it is inevitable that it will, entirely revolutionize all human life.

As an instrument of death, of course, it is appalling beyond description. As an instrument of life, though, it is possessed of limitless power of benefaction for the world at large . . .

We have unleashed a power which can, quite literally, destroy the earth.

We can never keep this power to ourselves, for what one nation has produced, any other nation can duplicate. And the potentialities of this new power as a weapon of war are so hideously great that it is simply unthinkable that the maddest of madmen would even tolerate the thought that there might be another way.

For the next war could have but one outcome: the suicide of the human race . . .

The harnessing of atomic power demands—and demands imperatively—the total disarmament of the entire world. It gives the final answer to peacetime conscription.

For the existence of arms and armies is no longer the threat to peace. It is a shameless acknowledgement that the nation which possesses them is evil, for it contemplates the possibility of a step which must inevitably destroy the race of men.

President Truman must summon an immediate meeting of the United Nations, and confront them with the true picture of international affairs, as it has now been changed so radically, and so dramatically.

No such meeting was called. The atomic bomb was used a second time, on Nagasaki, Japan.

"Sometimes many years must pass, and great volumes of wisdom added to our original source, before we comprehend the full content, before we are struck with the whole impact of that earlier disclosure. . . ."

By 1960, the proliferation of nuclear weapons had been such that stockpiles and delivery systems had been built adequate to destroy the world and human life more than a thousand times. Few, if any, safe uses of thermonuclear power had been developed.

Volumes of wisdom had not been added to the original disclosure.

Very little adjustment, political, economic, military, social and spiritual, had been made to the new Technological Revolution that was upon us.

✦ ✦ ✦

When we think of the 1960s, hard-edged images flood upon us, real for some of us who reported some of the scenes, filmic for all of us. Blacks being knocked over by fire hoses, dogs barking at them, because they no longer would sit in the back of the buses, eat lunch at a segregated counter, or be kept from state colleges. The saddled, black, cavorting horse, stirrups turned backwards, that followed John Kennedy's caisson through the streets of Washington. The sight and thwump-thwump-thwump of dark green helicopters scurrying over Indochinese jungle. The soundless sight of rows of filled, tagged body bags on the ground at an airbase in Vietnam, awaiting transportation home, there each to break a hundred hearts, to shatter a few good dreams. Tens of thousands of people marching in the streets to the beat of a slow, deep drum, singing John Lennon's simple melody, simple lyric, simple thought: "All we are saying . . . is give peace a chance."

By the 1960s, people worldwide were beginning to learn to use a new technology, particularly the medium of television, to enforce social adjustments, governmental and other institutional response, to the runaway Technological Revolution. We saw the size of Martin Luther King's marches grow. We saw Buddhist monks immolate themselves in protest against the Diem government of South Vietnam. We saw hundreds of thousands of people massed in protest against the war in Vietnam at the Washington Monument. "Even television distortion helps," said Youth International Party leader Paul Krasner. "Showing the freakiest people on television at a Yip-In for example, really helps. People viewing say, 'If someone can look that wild, then I can look a little weirder, freer than I do, and get away with it.'" During the riots outside the 1968 Democratic Convention in Chicago, demonstrators taunted the police with the chanted refrain: "The whole world is watching!"

From all this real and filmic memory comes the impression, I believe, that the cultural revolution of the 1960s was almost entirely a youth movement, a movement of the partially disenfranchised, the nearly voiceless minorities, the blacks, the women, the Hispanics, the impoverished, the homosexuals.

Such was not the case. The cultural revolution pervaded all American society. A case can be made that it pervaded all society, worldwide.

An observation that is frequently overlooked when reflecting upon the 1960s is that institutions were not really and ultimately caused to question themselves and the directions they were taking in the Technological Revolution by people rallying, sitting-in, marching in the streets, demonstrating peacefully, trashing buildings and burning neighborhoods. Political parties, churches, universities and other cultural institutions such as museums and symphony orchestras, private schools and clubs, were brought to their financial knees and forced to question their policies and practices ultimately by establishment people, who simply stopped writing checks.

The true story of the 1960s is not just that of a few people who learned how to manipulate computerized statistics back at the so-called establishment, or how to manipulate the media against media manipulators in power. As Richard Nixon was quoted as saying: "The people want to believe, don't they?"

The true story of the 1960s is also of tens of millions of people who never rallied, marched, demonstrated, chanted, or probably even consulted with each other. Individually, each of millions of Americans made a quiet decision: no longer were they going to volunteer their time and money to political parties, churches, universities and other institutions in which they no longer believed.

◆ ◆ ◆

And a generation after the 1960s, a general impression also surfaces occasionally that, in fact, the movements of that era were somehow isolated, frozen in time, and that in the long run not much was accomplished. Poverty was not abolished. The black Civil Rights Movement, although making some strides, got lost, entangled, aborted somehow in the Antiwar Movement. The Women's Movement did not result in an absolute parity in the workplace, or anywhere else. Homosexuals are still discriminated against violently. Children are still abused without much protection in the law. United States governments, employers, universities and other cultural institutions still cling to a categorical regard for human beings. The current statistic suggests that our governments and other institutions run a minimum of a dozen files on each of us, at a cost to us of about a thousand dollars per citizen. And there is still no guarantee that our governments will use the new technology of communications always before and instead of the new technology of thermonuclear weaponry.

Many reasonable, in fact essential, goals of the 1960s have not been achieved.

The question central to the Technological Revolution, what to do with and how to create parity among a rapidly increasing sector of worldwide population whose work product is not essential to human survival has not yet been addressed properly. Despair lies in believing the answers lie in the proliferation of drop-out drugs, crime statistics engorged by people sickened by their futility as individuals, or in the suicidal disposal of excess humans by thermonuclear war.

The 1960s were a threshold time. Bob Dylan's simple observation, "The times they are a-changing," may have been the understatement of all time. And John Kennedy's response, "Ask not what your country can do for you, but what you can do for your country," as it worked out, proved inadequate.

The answers to the Technological Revolution were not discovered in the 1960s, or early 1970s, nor have they been discovered yet.

But in the 1960s, some of the right questions began to be asked.

✦ ✦ ✦

The era of the 1960s ended a dozen times.

To some, it ended with the riots outside the Democrats' convention hall in Chicago, in 1968. For others, at the assassination of Martin Luther King in 1968. For others, at the assassination of Robert Kennedy in 1968. The era was over when Bob Dylan went into retirement; when the Beatles broke up; when Mick Jagger got married. It was over when a man first walked on the moon in 1969. The era was over at the Woodstock Music and Life Festival in Max Yasgur's pasture in the summer of 1969, which resulted, according to festival promoters, in ten thousand pregnancies. The era was over at the incident of murder by the Hell's Angels at the Rolling Stones' free concert at Altamont, California, in December 1969. The era of the 1960s was not over until the evacuation of Americans from Vietnam on April 29, 1974.

The people of that era—ah, the people. The people emerged out of the complacency of the 1950s like so many butterflies from cocoons, suddenly dawning bright, egalitarian clothing, wearing emblematic decorations and hairstyles never considered before, and found the courage of flight before overwhelming institutional machinery, essayed opinions and adventures, asked questions and made statements previously unthinkable. Tens of millions of individual revolutions took place.

It is the people, what they looked like, what they said and did, who, what, where, when, how and why, that are my souvenirs of a blown world.

These, then, are some of the people to whom I owe my education.

1   **Souvenirs of a Blown World**

On a beautiful fall Saturday afternoon, after a football game in Harvard Stadium, a kid in a red sweater and khaki pants rode in the back of a convertible through the streams of people pouring over Larz Anderson Bridge, up Boylston Street to Harvard Square, his loafered feet on the back seat, pretending he was a presidential candidate, pretending all this crowd was for him, waving to the people with the exuberance, confidence of a man on the way to the White House.

Some of the people noticed him, and with amusement, post-game silliness, waved back and cheered.

He was the only kid we ever knew who wanted to be president, had this dream, and of course we knew he would never make it, however rich and handsome, because he was Roman Catholic.

When the car stopped at the traffic light someone actually did shout, "Hi, Jack!" and the kid jumped to his feet to give a big, exuberant, hands-over-the-head wave. Just as the traffic light turned green and the car accelerated, someone else in the car tucked Jack in the ribs. Laughing at himself, Jack put his hands up to his face and fell sideways in the moving convertible, just as the Zapruder film was to show him doing on a November day in Dallas, Texas, years later.

To me, every time I have seen the Zapruder film, Jack Kennedy has been putting his hands up, falling sideways in the convertible, laughing at his own foolishness, and the foolishness of someone having tucked him in the ribs.

✦ ✦ ✦

The night Martin Luther King was shot I rode through the black ghetto in a taxi. I had been told to stay out of the ghetto that night.

The driver, who was in his sixties, insisted on going through the black district. "I ain't afraid of these black punks."

He told me he had a pistol on his hip.

Fire trucks passed us, American flags fluttering in the night above their front fenders. The idea of the flags was to make rock-throwers and snipers on the buildings' roofs think twice about aiming for the firemen whose job it was to put out the fires the black people had set in their own neighborhood.

In the back seat, I read a letter from a reader. She said she was going to kill me for something I had written about a popular singer. She wrote, "You may not believe me, but I'm serious." She signed her letter, "Love. . . ."

"Martin Luther King was already dead," a black friend said that night. "Today he just fell over."

To some, however desirable the result, there seemed a kind of repudiation of Doctor King in the extradition of his murderer, James Earl Ray, from England. In order to extradite Ray, the legal decision had to be made that Ray's murder of Martin Luther King had not been a political assassination, but just a murder.

Even in Doctor Martin Luther King's death, society found it necessary to abrogate him as a political leader.

◆ ◆ ◆

Riots really aren't very much, when you're in one. Thousands of people standing around, waiting, passing rumors, mostly spectating. To one side, in the television lights, maybe nine cops and five demonstrators mix it up, almost like a scrimmage at the side of a football field, something to do to relieve tension, to relieve boredom.

But when you're at home in Wyoming seeing the close-up of this scrimmage on television, hearing the reporter say that five, ten, fifty thousand people took part, you see the close-up of violence multiplied indefinitely, and you become very frightened for the world indeed.

✦ ✦ ✦

The day Robert Kennedy was shot, my wife, who listened to the morning radio news, left the house early and did not come back. She knew I had much work that had to be done that day.

After five, a friend of hers, a neighbor, dropped in unexpectedly to discuss with me the news I had not heard.

My wife arrived back during evening news, and together, we sat and watched this incredible reality on television, a medium which had brought us so much unreality.

✦ ✦ ✦

Kids with signs, Students for Humphrey, were being dragged forward, put in crowd scenes for photographers. A lotta youth for Humphrey. It was generally believed Hubert Humphrey, who had accomplished much for the Labor Movement in the United States, did not attract many young people to his campaign for president of the United States.

"Come on!" shouted an organizer. "Move those kids up there!"

Dutifully, a press photographer began to take their picture. "I bet they're sixty-year-old midgets," he muttered.

✦ ✦ ✦

During a recess in the trial to determine if the pediatrician/demonstrator Benjamin Spock was a good citizen, a gray-haired lady, well dressed, quite trim, who I had never seen before in my life, came up to me in the courthouse corridor and said, "How dare you prejudge me?"

Then she spat up into my face. Her spit landed on my right shoulder.

"That's all I have to say," she said.

And she walked off.

A young federal marshal, who had been standing nearby and watched the incident, shrugged. "I have no idea who she is," he said.

"And I'm sure she doesn't know who you are. That's just the way the country is now."

✦ ✦ ✦

Some kids in black leather jackets in the crowd behind me were being interviewed by a beery member of the international press.

"Hey, we gonna be on the news?"

"Why are you for George Wallace?"

"'Cause he stands up for America."

"Okay. Finally an answer I can print."

✦ ✦ ✦

A fast-stepping parade of Secret Service men came through the airplane door with the vice-presidential seal emblazoned on the inside and clumpety-clumped down the steps looking for all the world like an illustration from a child's book, all having the same builds, the same haircuts, the same suits, the same anxious, strained expressions on their faces.

The balding candidate came through the door of the plane, followed by his wife, waved, and then went down the steps into the mob looking precisely like an egg being lowered into boiling water.

One hand on my wallet, I rode into the mob in the wake of a 270-pound cop who smelled weirdly of cologne. In the moment it took me to get near the center of the mob, the top of the Humphrey egg had begun to bubble with sweat.

The mob then began to move as a body in the most incredible, awkward, inefficient, leg-clacking, sideways goose step around the front of the airplane, around a line of police cars, to the candidate's car.

The mob's centripetal force was such that the candidate's legs were not even moving. His trousers were perfectly slack. He was being hustled along at great speed, his head up, face smiling, one hand waving at the cameras. His eyes glanced down every few seconds nervously trying to see how far off the ground were his feet.

Smiling painfully, Muriel, the candidate's wife, was dragged past us at great speed, her whole body at an incredible angle to the ground. If dropped at that angle by the crowd, the Secret Service men could never have put her together again.

✦ ✦ ✦

Richard Nixon actually said: "Let's expand our Continental Shelf. . . ."

✦ ✦ ✦

"All you people who wish to participate in the silent vigil: Listen!

"Will you please sit down, and when Wallace says his first words, will you please stand up, turn around, and sit down again, your backs to him? Please?"

✦ ✦ ✦

Behind the bandstand at the political street-corner rally, hearing the roars of disapproval from the crowd was like hearing a sea storm from behind a breakwater.

Like mucous, volcanic sea mud the crowd squeezed up fainting ladies and lost, weeping children over the police barricades into the hands of white-coated doctors and nurses behind the bandstand.

On a wooden fence erected to save a department store's window glass, kids in blue jeans sat, spotting the desperate and the fallen among the crowd, waving their arms, pointing into the mob, directing the rescues of people politics had made momentarily breathless.

✦ ✦ ✦

A professor I respected very much said, "Two things have always happened prior to any dictatorship in any country. The first is a series of assassinations no one can quite explain. The second is that the sensitive people and the intellectuals, not being able to explain the assassinations logically to themselves, to accept them, disengage themselves from politics, government, society. However incredible the likelihood of a dictatorship happening here, these two things are happening."

That's the sort of thing that was being said at that time by reasonable, concerned people.

✦ ✦ ✦

Outside Faneuil Hall in Boston, the presidential candidate jumped out of a green Mercury convertible.

He was there to use Faneuil Hall as a photographic backdrop. The police fought the photographers off.

So the candidate escaped the police and waded into the small mob of shoppers to shake hands.

A plump, gray-haired lady carrying a shopping bag stood beside me on the doorstep of Faneuil Hall.

"Isn't this marvelous," she said, apparently to herself, or maybe to me. "It's so thrilling. Anybody could shoot him."

2   Pacem in Terris

*Jack Quiggly was hanging around his London flat, taking a loaf day,
when the phone rang.*

It was the recorded weather report, calling him.

When the weather report began the third time, he hung up.

*A few minutes later, the recorded weather report called him again.
He listened for a while and then hung up.*

*Every few minutes, the recorded weather report called him. If he
didn't answer, the telephone rang and rang and rang.*

He tried listening to the recorded weather report politely.

Shouting at it.

Glowering at the telephone.

Finally, in exasperation, he called the weather bureau to complain.

He got the recorded weather report.

*Which proves that you can initiate a meaningful dialogue with
anyone, even if you are just a recorded weather report.*

✦ ✦ ✦

*For the existence of arms and armies is no longer the threat to peace.
It is a shameless acknowledgement that the nation which possesses
them is evil, for it contemplates the possibility of a step which must
inevitably destroy the race of men.*

—Irving T. Mcdonald, August 7, 1945

✦ ✦ ✦

August 6, 1966, was the twenty-first anniversary of the bombing of
Hiroshima. There were to be peace walks around the world, and
around the world the newspapers were full of the wedding of the

daughter of the president of the United States, Luci Baines Johnson, to Patrick Nugent.

August 1966 was the month Russia invaded Czechoslovakia.

In Boston, it was a beautiful, sunny, warm, dry Saturday morning. At the bandstand on Boston Common there was a concert. Only a few tired shoppers and retired men sat on the benches in the shade listening.

At the edge of the circle of benches, partly in the sunlight, partly in the shade, mostly young people gathered, leaning their signs-on-sticks against the back of one bench. Defend Freedom with Nonviolent Resistance, read the top sign.

Boys and girls, dressed in shorts, cord trousers, pretty summer dresses, some were sixteen, some were twenty, some had knapsacks, introduced themselves to each other, and talked quietly.

The leader present, twenty-three-year-old Jim Hayes, was in full suit and tie.

There were two persons of sixty, a man and a woman, Andrew Farnsworth and Mrs. Rene Johnson, equally gracious in their regard for these young.

Policemen, a few, on horses, motorcycles, white helmeted, sat outside the group watching them. The band was thumping slowly an indistinguishable tune. A redheaded shoeshine boy went through the group looking for shoes to shine. There were only walking boots, sandals, moccasins. More youths arrived in work clothes and venerable Brooks Brothers suits. An amplified tape recorder from a church's clock tower sounded off a bell striking twelve.

"Let's move up to that monument," Jim Hayes said. "It's more open up there."

A middle-aged woman was standing at the fringe of the new crowd, looking at them with distaste. Under her arm was a copy of a weekly tabloid with the headline: Kills Son, Feeds Corpse to Pig.

The young people moved off toward the monument, some of them picking up the signs, everyone staying on the sidewalks except the press and the police, through two horse policemen, riot helmeted, making a gate. There was the initial roar of the motorcycles as they moved the few yards.

John Phillips, secretary of the Committee for Non-Violent Action, an indicted draft-card burner, stood on the step of the monument to the Boston Massacre and spoke. In nervousness, or fear, his voice quavered.

"We do not mean to criticize, or to make enemies, but rather to try a new experiment in reaching people."

The band music grew louder from the stand. Curious people stood in a circle, more than one hundred of them, waiting, listening.

"We hope you will join our peace walk to Provincetown."

Provincetown was more than 130 miles away.

Then Brad Little, New England coordinator of the committee, spoke. He too had the eyes of a very young, very earnest preacher.

A little man in a brown suit had placed himself behind the speakers. It was his intention to outshout the speakers. His sign, For God, Freedom and Country, Bomb Hanoi, Fight Communism and Communist Stooges, caused confusion. A practiced counterdemonstrator, he got himself, his sign, into every press photograph, every newsreel of the group.

His name was Josef Mlot-Mroz. He said he was a Polish Freedom Fighter.

"Communists! They're all Communist dupes!"

The next speaker, Tord Svenson, was less experienced at speaking to a rally than the previous two. Josef Mlot-Mroz was more successful in shouting him down.

The television cameras swung back and forth, as did the microphones.

"Lies, lies! He's lying. I'm telling you! Communist stooges!"

Svenson, voice quivering, said, "I am now going to destroy something. . . ."

The crowd tightened and backed off. The police moved closer. There were now 150 people and eighteen police.

Svenson took a cigarette lighter and three papers stapled together from his pocket.

His hands shaking, the crowd watching wide-eyed, Tord Svenson set fire to his National Guard honorable discharge papers, holding them between his fingers until they burned him.

Then he dropped the black, curled papers, ashes, to the sidewalk.

A man at the front of the crowd, hands on the shoulders of his small son, said, in genuine shock, "You *are* a traitor!"

Svenson had spent six years in the National Guard Reserve, six months on active duty. He had never seen actual fighting.

A gesture, a legal, meaningless gesture, done with fear, angered the crowd. "Coward! You traitor!"

The crowd pressed forward again, to scream at Svenson, to shake fists.

The son, frightened, feeling his father's shock and anger through the hands on his shoulders, said, "That's right."

The man said, "There's a boat right now at Commonwealth Pier. Why don't you get on it?"

Jim Hayes shouted, "Would all walkers please form a single line to the right? Please stay in a single line."

Leaving the sound of the band music in the green park, the roar of the motorcycles with them, the peace walkers crossed Tremont Street in single file, and down Winter Street. The police scooted ahead to close off cross-traffic.

A young person walked at the head of the single line carrying the sign Pacem in Terris, Peace on Earth. Behind him, two men carried an enlarged photograph: dead, mutilated Oriental bodies in a pile.

"Hey," said a horse policeman to one of the fifty-five peace walkers. "Are you going through Hyannis? You ought to go through Hyannis. It's nice down there."

At the corner of Washington Street, Saturday shoppers in light summer clothes watched the single line file past, down Summer Street, seeing the peace walkers as one more big city oddity.

A girl walking in the line behind a boy of fifteen said, "Ben, you're not going to walk through the South End, are you? They'll kill you."

Fight Poverty, Not People, read another sign.

At South Station, airline-struck railroad travellers were the first to smile.

Uniformed foot police left the walkers at the sunny corner of South Station, in Martell-Munro Square. Only the police cars and motorcycles were to continue.

Five plainclothesmen were not sure. "I guess we should walk as far as the bridge," decided the oldest.

Behind South Station, baggage handlers yelled through the ports. Yelled one, "How about a pamphlet?"

"I got some," Josh Kricker said, starting to walk over to the baggage ports. Sixteen years old, Josh had just been released from reform school for demonstrating against the nuclear submarine called *Will Rogers*.

"Get out of here!" yelled the same man. "Private property! Give me a pamphlet!"

He reached down and took a pamphlet from Josh and hurled it to the ground.

Walk for Peace.

"Plans changed," Pris Curtis told us. "We're walking twelve miles today instead of five."

✦ ✦ ✦

We went ahead and waited for them inside P. F. Connelly's Bar, at the corner of Boston Street and Dorchester Avenue. There was a cool breeze through the three doors. Workmen, some playing dominoes, others just talking, were drinking cold beer on a hot day. Over the bar was a picture of John F. Kennedy.

When the television cameramen came in from their station wagon for a cold beer, the bartender got wise and cleaned all the empty bottles, glasses off the bar.

The sound of the motorcycles brought the men to stand in the bar's doors.

The thin, straggly line of peace walkers entered Andrew Square. Refuse to Pay Taxes for War.

"Cowards. Look at the hair on 'em."

"Is that a girl or a boy with them?"

"They're afraid to go out and fight."

"How many of them are veterans?"

There was a debate inside the bar then, with beer, about Vietnam. Then, questions about the people walking.

"Provincetown? How are they going to do it?"

"On the expressway?"

"Where are they going to camp out?"

"That takes more guts than being in Vietnam," one guy said. "Walking through here."

✦ ✦ ✦

"Now you learn the truth!" Josef Mlot-Mroz said.

He revealed a new sign: Communism is Jewish (Zionist) from Start to Finish! Smash Communism Everywhere! Polish Freedom Fighters, Inc.

He let little boys hold his old sign.

"Brian! John!" A mother ran across the road. "Come away from there. Don't take their picture, mister." She took Mlot-Mroz's signs away from them, dropping them in the road. "What if your Aunt Marie saw you?"

A shiny, new, red Chevrolet with streamers broke through the peace walkers at an intersection, honking its horn: a Saturday wedding.

LOVE NOT HATE.

Thirty-seven men were outside Johnny Cunningham's Bar and Grill, on the sidewalk, arms folded, arms akimbo, veterans all, or most all. There was hatred in their faces. Outside the Peter and Dick Tavern there were only fourteen.

"Chickens!" they yelled. "Cowards!"

A group of neighborhood boys, a gang, decided to follow the peace walkers. "Let's stay with them," said one in shorts. "They're a bunch of dips."

There were many men outside Foley's Tavern, three o'clock beery. "Cowards!" Fists shaking; temple veins showing. "Love it or leave it!"

The bartenders, bouncers, probably for the first time in history, were trying to bounce the men back into the tavern.

"What are they against?" asked a little kid on the sidewalk.

"They're against war."

"Isn't everybody?"

The Boston contingent, not quite half of the fifty-five walkers, left at Fields Corner by prearrangement to take the subway back to town.

Along Neponset Avenue, the fifteen neighborhood boys, the gang, kept pace with the peace walkers on the opposite sidewalk, yelling at them over the noise of the traffic, the police cars, the press cars. Past Saint Anne's School, the green statue of the Madonna. Past the empty William H. Garvey Playground.

The Boston Police asked the peace walkers to wait on Neponset Bridge for the Quincy Police.

Then past the Sheraton Motor Inn.

The neighborhood gang had picked up some raw eggs and were throwing them at the peace walkers. They hit none. The eggs were splattering on the road, the sidewalks, the sides of buildings.

A motorcycle policeman asked them to stop and they did. They were out of eggs.

At the request of the police, the peace walkers rested outside the Quincy police station, to wait for the night shift.

Across the street, at a gas station, was a big soft-drink machine. As soon as some of the peace walkers headed for the soft-drink machine, the neighborhood gang, arms folded across their chests, blocked it off.

Sitting on the wall in front of the police station, Mrs. Rene Walker said, "I think they should be allowed to throw eggs. They should be able to express themselves, too."

"If the cops weren't here, we'd kick you in the root," a kid yelled at her.

"But I'm really very thirsty," she said quietly.

Having rendered the soft-drink machine inoperable, the gang crossed the street to the patch of lawn in front of the police station where the peace walkers rested.

"Hey, Bucket," said one. "Too bad about your brother getting killed in Vietnam."

"Yeah, ain't it?"

They grabbed the pamphlets and ripped them up. They strew the pieces around the ground.

"Why not throw them into Vietnam?"

"They stick behind college doors and grow beards."

A peace walker said, "Why do you say beards? I'm the only one here with a beard."

Mrs. Johnson signalled him to be quiet. Standing on the sidewalk with his sign, Josef Mlot-Mroz kept up his yelling at them: "Communist dupes!"

Before the walk resumed, the gang tried to break the main sign, to kick Pacem in Terris to pieces. The police, the night shift, yelled at them to stop, and they did stop.

Down Route 3A, past the A&P, the Quincy Lumber Yard, the Roman Gardens.

"Liars! Communist dupes!"

Another older man was now following the peace walkers, yelling the same things at them Josef Mlot-Mroz was yelling. "You fools! You Communists!"

His name was Oscar Blumit. He said he was Jewish, and that he had been a prisoner in a Nazi concentration camp.

Josef Mlot-Mroz, yelling and carrying his anti-Semitic sign, and

Oscar Blumit, yelling and shaking his fists, followed the peace walkers all the way to the rotary in front of the General Dynamics Plant.

In front of the General Dynamics main gate, the peace walkers lined up with their signs, in silent demonstration.

"Communists!" shouted Josef Mlot-Mroz.

"Dupes!" shouted Oscar Blumit. "Traitors!"

The cars which were supposed to meet the peace walkers and pick them up at the General Dynamics gate were not there. And they did not come. One had broken down and the other was stuck in traffic.

Across the rotary, the gang of boys were held at bay by one motorcycle policeman.

People going by in cars yelled at the gang of kids, "Get 'em! Go after 'em! Kill 'em!"

Finally, one of the gang sneaked by the motorcycle policeman and, with a sneakered foot, kicked Pacem in Terris to pieces.

A foot patrolman grabbed the kid by the T-shirt and threw him to the ground.

Jim Hayes asked that the kid be released. Andrew Farnsworth asked that the kid be released. Mrs. Rene Johnson asked that the kid be released.

The police released the kid.

From across the rotary, the kid yelled back at the peace walkers, "Chickens!"

"Communists!"

"Dupes!"

Nearly an hour had gone by and there was no sign of the cars that were to pick up the peace walkers and transport them to where they were to camp that night.

Oscar Blumit walked away, back the way he had come.

Shortly, Josef Mlot-Mroz, after a few more unchallenged yells, carried his sign away, up the street.

The crowd across the rotary was getting larger.

Cars were circling the rotary again and again. People were yelling out the car windows, "Kill the yellow bastards! Kill the goddamn Commies!"

Again a young man, whom the police had warned several times, broke through the police line. He was swinging at the demonstrators.

The police subdued him and put him in the back of a police car to take to the station.

A Mercedes-Benz entered the rotary, drove around to the demonstrators, and stopped. Inside were Oscar Blumit and Josef Mlot-Mroz.

The anti-Semite and the Jewish victim of Nazism in the Mercedes-Benz offered to transport the peace walkers to wherever they planned to camp that night.

Six of the peace walkers were able to fit in the car that first trip.

The Mercedes-Benz drove off toward Wollaston, with all these signs sticking out the windows

3 Jack Kerouac

You have to be crazy to be a writer in this country!
—Jack Kerouac

✦ ✦ ✦

The house in Hyannis had already been let and there was a For Sale sign plastered on the development house in Lowell.

In what was designed to be the dining room of that house lay his mother, the skin of her face as smooth as a baby's, her left side paralyzed by a stroke two years before. All she wanted was to move to St. Petersburg, Florida, where a house was waiting for them.

"I know Jackie's trying very hard to get some money, but I don't know."

A few feet away, in the living room, just the other side of a thin, plastic, folding accordion door, facing the other way, sat Jack Kerouac in a rocking chair, red slippers, white socks, pajama pants, open plaid flannel shirt, T-shirt over a big belly, still-bigger chest, not having shaved or eaten for four days, not since we had arranged to do this thing, "completely surrounded by booze," in his own words, averaging twelve to fifteen shots of whiskey and gulps of beer an hour, seven feet from his own television, staring at the midday pap, his mind as sensitive as a frog's open heart, talking.

"If I didn't have my Scotch and beer I wouldn't speak to anybody."

Over the mantelpiece, to the right of his television, was a fine pencil drawing of his brother, who died at the age of nine of rheumatic fever, done by a German. The drawing was on the cover of a

Kerouac book, *Visions of Gerard,* "which nobody reads anymore. It's too sad."

On the wall behind Kerouac was a painting called *Night Wash,* done by a friend, which was exactly that, a literal pun. Directly over his head was a painting of Pope Paul as a cardinal (copied from *Life* magazine eight years previously) by Kerouac himself.

"Painting's my hobby. I don't like to do it. It makes my hands dirty."

In the background, the present Mrs. Kerouac, Stella, looking old enough to be everybody's mother (Jack's first marriage was annulled; his second ended in divorce; he was married for the third time in Hyannis, November 1966), moved from the dining room to the kitchen to the living room, nursing them both, getting coffee for me, helping things to be understood, arranging for the lawn to be fertilized, giving Greek cookies to a young man who came to the door, for his mother, collecting what photographs they had for me to use with this story.

"I absolutely will not be photographed," Kerouac said.

"It's all right, Jackie," Stella said. "There will be no photographers. He promised."

She had told me that the previous winter a reporter and photographer from *Newsweek* magazine had worked with Kerouac for hours. He had even splashed around, fully dressed, in a stream in which the ice was just breaking, snow still on the banks, for the camera.

As a result he was ill for months.

And *Newsweek* never used the story, or photographs.

"I guess I wouldn't have made a soldier. My theory is to give all the soldiers belts with bottles of whiskey hanging from them. That way they'd win the battle. Makes you sentimental. Everybody would look out for his buddy."

Two months before, his brother-in-law, who had been a World War II army sergeant, went on a sentimental trip back to Europe.

He took the great novelist Kerouac with him, thinking that way he would get red-carpet treatment everywhere he went.

They were thrown out of several places.

Among other things, Jack paid a prostitute in Portugal named Linda ten dollars to stare into his eyes for a solid hour by the clock. Then he gave her another ten.

In Germany, Kerouac became fascinated by the way the "Aryan types" walked along the street.

He got up to strut, march, goose step with himself up and down the living room sixteen times in hilarious imitation. The narrow, modern living room was full of the movement of this 190-pound bear of a man.

"I came back to America saying, the poor Jews."

In his chair again, staring at the continuous daytime pap, taking constant Scotch and beer: "I want to be commissioned to do my next book, which will be called *Beat Spotlight*. I want $5000 advance on that and $5000 advance on *Visions of Cody* so I can get the hell out of here and get to Florida. The people here are nice. The water's no good."

His last book, published only a few months previously by Coward-McCann, *Vanity of Duluoz* (three syllables: Du-lu-oz: the louse; Kerouac: the cockroach), is autobiography, from his Lowell boyhood to prep school in New York, Columbia University, the Navy, the Merchant Marine, to the point where he went on the road. It's a good book.

About ten percent of *Cody* had been published in a limited edition in 1960.

"*The Complete Visions of Cody*. Not published yet. I wrote it sixteen years ago, in 1952. Ginsberg told me it's the masterpiece of all ages. It's a fantastic poem. A five-hundred-and-twelve-page paean to a cowboy I once knew, Cody, whose real name is Neal Cassady, who was the Moriarty in *On the Road*. I've changed his name now four or five times.

"You know, a little magazine on the West Coast is saying that he died trying to live up to the image I created for him. A crock of shit. The fact is, he's not even dead. It's a trick."

"Jack, you don't know he's not dead," Stella said. "His wife said so."

"I think he's in Spain. Mexico's a big place, too. It's just a trick to get out from under his wife."

"You'll see him, Jack."

"I don't mean transcendental things. I think he might be dead. Last time I saw him he was ranting. Do you want to hear how he talked?"

Jack then did an imitation of how Cassady had talked four years before: irrationally.

"I said, 'Why haven't you changed, Cassady? You're still stupid!' He was losing control. They got him a bus, flowers painted all over it that said Nowhere on it. And he drove the bus from California to New Orleans to New York. With fifty couples playing guitars and throwing flowers out the windows. They had a microphone in front of his face and he talked all the way, onto tape, from California to New York. No wonder he went mad.

"We met Ginsberg in the East Village and he said, 'Let's go to a party,' and I said, 'Who's going to be there?' and Ginsberg said, 'Ken Kesey, there are movies and lights and dancing on the flag.' Ginsberg put the flag around my shoulders and I took it off and folded it up and put it over the sofa. I was disgusted and I still am.

"America was an idea that was proposed and began to deteriorate at the turn of the century when people came in waving flags. And now their grandchildren dance on the flag. Damn them."

Reading Kerouac's great books of the Beat Generation, *On the Road, The Dharma Bums, Big Sur,* you had to wonder what would happen to the characters therein, to the leaders of any exuberant, youth-freedom movement once youth was gone, fifteen years later.

"Neal Cassady's wife, Carolyn, called Jack February fourth, a few months ago, and told him they had found Neal dead beside a rail-road track in Mexico," Stella said to me. "Coincidentally enough, February fourth is his mother's, Memere's, birthday."

In 1971, the very unfinished writings of Neal Cassady were to be published by City Lights, called *The First Third,* a partial autobiography.

And the first third of that book is wonderful.

According to Kerouac's own account, he himself had written eighteen books, which had been translated into eighteen languages and published in forty-three countries.

His income that year, the year he was forty-six, averaged $60 a week. The most he ever made from a book was $40,000, off *On the Road*, which was taxed as straight income. Much of the rest was used paying for his mother's interminable north-south-north moves. Only *The Subterraneans* was bought for a movie, from which he profited little.

"Why should they buy *On The Road* when they can steal it?" Stella asked. "Did you ever see that television program, 'Route 66'?"

Jack said, "In New York it is quite common to make light of someone who is honest and not demanding."

In that morning's mail had been a letter from his agent saying Kerouac owed him $157.

There had also been a letter from some creeps in Oregon saying they were going to have a seance to contact the spirit of Neal Cassady, and it might be easier for them if Kerouac were there.

When his wife read this letter to him, Kerouac shrieked: "On my magic carpet I will fly!"

He jumped up. "I want you to note that besides being a great painter and a great writer, I'm a great pianist and composer."

He then sat at the upright piano.

"You'll only wake up Memere, Jack."

And played notes and chords. "'God Rest Ye Merry, Gentlemen' is a Cornish folk tune," he said. "I'm Cornish."

"He saw a Cornish movie on television last night," Stella said. "With Rex Harrison."

He sat in his rocker again.

I asked why he had never spent much time in Europe.

He put his head in his hands.

He said slowly, "I'd like to have a little farm in southern France, like Picasso."

I should have told you before this that every time Kerouac spoke, with self-consciousness, he used a different accent, high British, Cockney, Southern, Irish, Southwestern.

"Why don't you tell him the truth, Jack, why you've never lived in Europe?"

He stood up, heavily.

"Because I'm an American pioneer."

He went upstairs.

She said, "He can't get enough of it, that's all."

He came back down the stairs with two slim boxes in his hand.

"You want to know why I like America. I'll tell you why."

Sitting in his rocker, hunched over, eyes closed, he played "Across the Wide Missouri" on one of the two harmonicas so sweetly in the midday shade of the room it would have made Mao love America.

He played a sort of flamenco on the other harmonica.

"That covers Mexico," he said.

And "O Canada" on the first harmonica, sort of wetly.

"And that covers Canada."

"He just can't get enough of it," Stella said. "This country."

"The American Civil Liberties Union is Communist. The police are afraid to arrest genuine malefactors," he shouted.

He opened the window behind my head and gently waved a bug through it.

"My brother taught me that," he said, indicating the drawing of the nine-year-old boy over the fireplace.

"All they arrest is harmless drunks like me!

"I came to Lowell because I thought I was coming home again. America used to be a pretty good country. Kids used to hang themselves at Camp Lee in 1942 to '43, rather than be sent overseas."

Much of Kerouac's short time in the service was spent in a naval mental hospital. Any real action he saw was in the Merchant Marine.

From his rocker, he pointed to my car through the window.

"Is that your car? I can drive, but I've never had a license. I can drive on the highway, but not downtown. All my friends are the best drivers. Neal driving me three thousand miles across the country, all the time looking me in the eyes.

"I'm afraid of cars. I'm not afraid of horses. Horses can fight back. Cars might hit somebody."

He then did an imitation, complete with mouth noises of horses' hoof beats, of a lancer on a horse.

"I'm afraid of all machines. I have machinophobia. My mother can only sleep in the back seat when I'm at the wheel."

The family car was a thirteen-year-old black Ford coupe, in the driveway.

"How do you write?" I asked. "Is it much trouble for you to get yourself up for it?"

"As Saint Matthew says, 'Do not store up in your mind what you will say, for it is the Holy Ghost who speaks through you.' I don't write. The Holy Ghost writes through me. You're surprised, aren't you? This is the first time you've ever met the Holy Ghost in person. I do a certain mechanical thing. But I am the Holy Ghost speaking."

"What purpose are you serving through the Holy Ghost?"

"I'm taking orders from heaven. In heaven sits God. On his left, Mary. On his right, Jesus. In front of them, the golden baby of paradise: Jackie Kerouac. I have a high opinion of myself, right? I'm serious. I was sent here to do something."

"What are you doing?"

"I'm a messenger. I didn't want to come here. May I remind you that you have never seen my Father's face? I have seen his face. I am the brother of Jesus. We're a very holy family."

"Incidentally, my mother is a descendant of Napoleon."

"You're the messenger. What's the message?"

"The message from heaven? That after we die we're all raised to the highest part of heaven, no matter what we do, as a fitting reward to answer Lucifer's plea to fall from heaven. Lucifer comes to us in heaven, you see, and says, 'You like it up here, Jackie? Couldn't things be better?' You say, 'Yeah, maybe,' and *Tha-wong!* you're born. But it couldn't be better. Beds of roses. Clouds making refreshing faces all day long."

He looked at me most seriously, as if to scold me.

He said, "Religion, *señor*, is your own broken heart.

"You think I'm insane, don't you? I am insane. All American authors are insane. You have to be crazy to be a writer in this country!"

While Kerouac tried to get his agent on the phone (his agent was "out of the country" that day) I talked with Jack's mother about Florida and looked at some paintings Stella brought up from the basement, one by Gregory Corso, six or seven by Jack Kerouac, one of which was bright and happy. Stella said he had done it while on mescaline.

Jack then called his publisher: "Give me $5000 on *Complete Visions of Cody* and $5000 on *Beat Spotlight* so I can get my mother to Florida and get to work on *Beat Spotlight*. Listen. Give me no money. Just publish *Complete Visions of Cody*. Ginsberg says it's an important book."

Jack then allowed me to understand the publishers are not too keen on *The Complete Visions of Cody*.

"It's always been too dirty," he said.

Stella tried to induce him to stay home by reminding him that "The Merv Griffin Show" started at four-thirty. While I had been upstairs for a minute, Jack had sort of dressed in trousers, shoes, a wind breaker and a porkpie hat.

On the sidewalk he screamed at kids playing basketball in the next driveway to shut up and when they looked terrified at him he gave them the raspberry.

In the car, I said, "How come you've never been able to finish anything, a year of school, a football season, yet you have been able to finish so many books?"

"I don't finish. I just write it continuously. Sooner or later you reach the point in a book where you feel everybody's bored, and you bring it around somehow and end it. That's deep form."

He entered every bar shouting ferociously: "I'm Kerouac!"

In every bar in Lowell, following his nose sideways across every street, Kerouac is known.

"When you first thought of writing, when you were a kid, what kind of a writer did you think you were going to be?"

"I thought I was going to be Mark Twain."

"In your own mind, what kind of a writer are you?"

"A naturalistic. Like Dreiser. A German Romanticist. Write 'em both down. A Celtic twilight."

"Anybody writing today better than you are?"

"No. Not since Shakespeare. When he went out for a beer in the afternoon, people called him Sweet Will. They should call me Sweet Jack. Except maybe Laurence Sterne." Beside his chair at the house was a book by Laurence Sterne. "Maybe George Herbert."

He had taken $5 from his wife before he left the house. Second bar we were in he gave a kid named Morris $1 for shining his shoes.

"What do you think of Norman Mailer?"

"He's an ugly and ridiculous man."

To everybody's amusement and disdain, watering the corner of nearly every redbrick building we passed, Kerouac pursued sleep through every bar in Lowell.

At some point in our progress, a kindly cop named Pasquale, "Pat," cigar held in a toothless gap in the front of his mouth, told me about the time Jack had seen three pedigreed dogs through a pet shop window, a malamute, a collie and something else, and had bought all three at once, to have them drag him through the bars.

"What were you so vain about, Duluoz?"

"Beating everybody athletically and by scholarship."

He recited Emily Dickinson in the green bars, most of which looked like stage sets for a play by William Alfred, shamrocks every-where, tall and short men called Councilor, Commissioner, in shiny suits standing up at the bar, talking about ward politics, who is in, who is out, and of jail, who is in, who is out, scowling at the half-staffed trousers of this man they grew up with who carries a bit of the world (he knows where Oregon is, and Oregon knows where he is) and a lot of books on the weight of his breath.

"What would have happened to you Jack, if you had never left Lowell?"

"I would have worked in a mill all my life."

He shouted nonsense tone poems of his own (Beejeebeejeebee), the personal meanings of which brought tears to his own eyes, wide set, gray-blue, as different from each other as the tragicomic masks, and pleadingly expressive.

He took literary advice from everybody we met, every cop, fly and broad, that he should write, and when, and about what, saying only, each time, his wide and handsome grin beneath four days' stubble: "You know what? It's weird, but what he says is true."

What he wanted to fight about was whether Al Mello was the best boxer ever to come out of Lowell.

The first time he punched me, he had the preppy's grace to grab his workman's square, intellectual's soft hand and say, "Ouch!" as if he meant it, and the second time he hit me more softly.

I think he wanted to say that he had been the best boxer, the best anything, to have come out of Lowell.

Then he sprayed me with wet laughter.

"Have you ever felt one-to-one with anyone, Jack?"

"Yes. Neal Cassady. He can't be dead. Oh, God. He can't be dead."

At the house he had said, "I don't speak with an accent all the time. I've got to get out of here."

"Have you ever been yourself with anyone, Jack?"

"I know another bar."

I was to leave him, asleep, sitting at a bar owned by his brother-in-law.

"Religion, *señor*, is your own broken heart."

"What about it?"

"That's a beautiful line, Sweet Jack."

Fourteen months later, Jack Kerouac died of a hemorrhage, in Florida.

4 Claude Smith

My theory is to give all the soldiers belts with bottles of whiskey hanging from them. That way they'd win the battle. Makes you sentimental. Everybody would look out for his buddy.

—Jack Kerouac

✦ ✦ ✦

We were drinking Scotch in milk at a small table in a waterfront dive, soldier Claude Smith and I. He was all pressed and shining in a new uniform, new ribbons, his wounds freshly dressed, these few days before his discharge.

After a long time, after two or three phone calls to the public relations officer at his army base to make sure it was really all right to tell me his story, he began talking, slowly at first.

✦ ✦ ✦

We had been riding since six a.m., sixteen troop carriers, tracks, coming out of the base at Cu Chi, over Ann-Margret Bridge onto the straight, narrow, jungle road, toward Saigon, twenty miles away, northwest, single file. The sound of the wheels through the steel walls of the truck was like the whir of hand lawnmowers going fast, steady at our top speed, forty-five miles per hour.

Van's troop carrier was behind us and when we wheeled left and fanned into the jungle, wedge formation, his track was to the left, a little behind us.

Sweeping the jungle, the lawnmower sounds of the sixteen tracks whirred up and down as they plowed through the weeds, over stumps.

We took turns manning the fifty caliber in the turret hatch and the regular sixty in the rear.

There were supposed to be eleven of us in the track, but there were only eight. We had had losses.

In Van's track, there were seven.

Through noon the jungle temperature was ninety-five degrees. Inside the troop carrier it was 120.

There was the heat and the noise of the wheels we had to shout over to be heard, and the sweat, anyway.

Sitting, his back against the wall, Munroe said, "Smith decided to come with us this time. So we're all safe, right, Smitty?"

"He didn't have no intuition this time," said Love.

It actually made them feel better I was there, this time.

"If Smith says it's a piece of cake, it's a piece of cake," Munroe said. "I believe it."

A few weeks before I had been told I would be court-martialed.

I had been out on patrol too much, you see, and that night I knew I was going to die if I went out. I knew it.

O'Brien had been with us a short while. He was with us at Cu Chi. We liked that boy.

He pulled a grenade with a short fuse. Grenades are supposed to have eight-second fuses, but there was no eight seconds on that one. No one could have gotten it off.

He pulled the pin and it blew him up.

Whether or not there are eight seconds on a fuse is up to the manufacturer.

There had been Billy Brown Day. That boy had twenty-four hours left in Vietnam.

I had said, "Sit this one out, man. You don't need it."

On that patrol I was feeding ammo to his 60.

He just said, "Goddamn," like that, quiet, like he had jammed his finger, and fell back on me.

A bullet had gone through his forehead.

The sergeant made me go to the colonel to tell him I wasn't going out that night.

"You're a good soldier, Smith," the colonel said.

"I'm not going out. I'd die tonight. I know that."

"It's eight o'clock," he said. "The patrol goes over that bridge at twelve. If you're not with it, court-martial. You have four hours to decide."

"I don't need no four hours to pack for court-martial."

Vickers was no cherry colonel. He had been in this war a long time. And he knew me from training in Hawaii and all this action here at Cu Chi.

He held the patrol a few minutes, to give me extra time.

I didn't need extra time. I was in my foxhole, sitting on my pack, dressed for court-martial. Too many already had died. I would rather be in jail.

In fact, I had already been busted in Hawaii. I went AWOL on New Year's Eve. Then I went AWOL again when I was on restriction. What did I care about that? They said I would never get rank. I was on K.P. when I arrived in Saigon Harbor. Eighteen days of it, all the way from Hawaii.

At twelve o'clock exactly that bridge was blown up by the Viet Cong.

The whole battalion would have got it.

Nothing more was ever said about the court-martial.

People, Vickers, just looked at me.

Everybody really felt better on the next patrols when I was with them.

"So we're pretty safe," said Munroe.

"No wonder we ain't found nothin' yet. Your antenna must be working, Smitty."

I took the turret hatch for a while.

Someone else was in the turret hatch of Van's troop carrier. We didn't smile to each other or wave.

We just plowed through the weeds.

Up in the air of the hatch you sweat more than in the truck.

If the gooks are in the weeds, we roll over them, anything, kill them. Mostly they are in the trees.

This whole area was our area. We had made it ours.

Big Red One was supposed to have secured Cu Chi for us. It was our first assignment. After four days in Vietnam, four days in a camp outside Saigon University, we had to fight our way into the town of Cu Chi and through it to the base. The area had not been secured. When we got there, Big Red One had to pull out, go work some other area.

In Cu Chi base we were hit every few minutes. Snipers could shoot into camp from far away. We had 'holes, but we would be hit just walking around, going to the latrine. Even picking up food there would be one in a tree right over us, waiting for us to put down our rifles. We would have to drop our food in the mud and shoot the leaves. Gooks tie themselves to the trees so they won't fall out when they're hit. We were never sure we had made a kill unless someone climbed the tree. We stayed on rations three months. We lost I don't know how many men, walking around.

Along the side of the base opposite the town ran a river, and we had to fight for that. First, we needed the water. We strung a rope high across the river and went across it dangling from our hands.

A lot were shot and dropped into the river.

We secured a little area on the other side. Then we built a bridge so the troop carriers could get across and in two or three months were able to secure a much larger area.

There had been a lot of gooks in that area, and we had really made it ours. We even built an outpost, far on the other side of the river.

Ann-Margret entertained in Saigon. She's a beautiful girl. She was the only one who ever came to see us at Cu Chi. We loved that girl, all of us; we really appreciated her. We named everything after her, the bridge, the outpost. Ann-Margret Bridge. Ann-Margret Outpost. Ann-Margret Everything.

Then cherry green troops came in.

It was their job to keep the area we had secured clear while we rode helicopters, but they were cherry, didn't know what they were doing. They hadn't fought for the area so they let much of it go. They sent out two patrols when they should have had thirty sweeping the area.

Of course the gooks infiltrated. They're real ribbon-happy. They are brave.

And they are brilliant. They can make an explosive out of something as small as a cigarette filter. They're good soldiers.

Of course, they're fighting for something that means something to them.

When we caught a gook we would try to keep him away from the South Vietnamese. We knew what would happen to him.

So we had been sent out to patrol the area again. All day we had seen nothing.

The lieutenant signalled stop. Everybody could get out, cool off, relieve himself. It was three o'clock in the afternoon. He was cherry, a good man, but cherry. The cargo hatches were put down, but some of the men did not get out. They were not cherry.

I went to talk to Van.

"Listen," Van said, sweating. "We'll have a ball. Think about it." Van Cleef was from New York and I was from Boston. We planned to have parties in each other's cities on alternate weekends when we got home. Van Cleef was white who didn't know what color-talk was. A gentleman from Brooklyn, New York.

I knew I wouldn't go down unless Van went down too. I didn't expect Van would go down without my going down.

"Keep thinking about it," Van said.

"Might as well mount up and go home," the lieutenant said. "We're not finding anything."

He said, "Hot."

"Yes, sir," Van Cleef said.

"We might as well go home."

The lieutenant went back to the center track. Cargo hatches began to close.

We didn't know they were looking at us, right then.

"It'll be much cooler in New York, baby," Van said. "The Village."

"We'll make it cool in Boston. Real cool."

"Think on it," Van said.

The cargo hatches were up but it seemed we really hadn't started to move, a little bit maybe, when there was fire from everywhere.

They hit us too hard.

Love was in the turret at the 50, and I was feeding ammo to Castro at the 60 in the cargo hatch. Someone else was working the M-16 through the hatch.

They must have been a whole battalion.

"They don't make sense."

All we could do was spray the trees. We could never see anybody.

"Why didn't they hit us when we were stopped? When we were outside? Damn, they don't make sense."

I heard Love screaming that the 50 had jammed and went to pull his ammo belt.

"Hit it, baby," I said.

There was a great explosion from our left, a little behind us, and right away another one just beside us.

We must have stopped on top of detonator mines and activated them the second we moved. It felt like a giant thing was standing right next to our track, shaking us.

"Damn them! Van!"

I tried to get up to the turret to see what had happened.

Something slammed my head, knocking me towards a wall. My helmet came off.

Later we found a bullet in it.

Before I hit the wall, shrapnel cut into my left cheek, right leg, and inside my right ear.

My blood hit the wall sooner than I did.

"Van!"

The troop carrier engined and swung to the right, clear of the area.

"No," I said. "Van."

We ran a few minutes, perhaps a mile, until the firing stopped. I knew all the tracks would have scattered.

We stopped.

Love came down and looked at the mess of blood I had made.

"Baby, you're wounded, but we've got to go back."

I couldn't hear him right away.

"We've got to go back," I said. "We've got to see what happened to Van."

He said, "We've got to go back to see if anybody's left."

We engined up and swung back to the area.

When we stopped again there wasn't a sound. Just the jungle noises again, faintly.

The whole battalion had gone.

"What happened?" I said.

Two of them helped me up to the turret. My legs wouldn't hurry enough.

Three wheels were left. Things were hanging from the trees in the peculiar silence. Van Cleef.

I couldn't even say, "Jesus."

Back across the bridge they brought me towards a different door of the dispensary, not the one I had been through before, for pills. This was the wounded door.

I didn't want to go through that door.

Along the wall beside that door to the dispensary, the seven ponchos had already been lined up.

There wasn't enough in any of them even to serve on a plate.

They would all be reported Missing In Action.

Jesus.

I couldn't even say, "Jesus."

5   John Wayne

The worst bartender in the worst bar in the worst section of the most dead-end city in the United States said, "Fifty-two percent of American males get to a certain point in their drinking and become John Wayne. They stand like him, hitch their pants like him, talk like him."

"What do the other forty-eight percent become at that point?" I asked.

"Sick."

✦ ✦ ✦

Of course the gooks infiltrated. They're real ribbon-happy. They are brave.

And they are brilliant. They can make an explosive out of something as small as a cigarette filter. They're good soldiers.

Of course, they're fighting for something that means something to them.

—Claude Smith

✦ ✦ ✦

It was midnight and we were under an adobe arch beside a swimming pool on a ranch outside Dallas, Texas, and Big John Wayne was wearing his head rug, a loose khaki shirt, and pants pressed like I had never seen pants pressed before—all the way up to his belt in back.

There was to be a world premiere of his two hundred and first movie, *Chisum*, in Dallas the next day, a parade to a new theater, a speech by Governor Preston Smith, a presentation to John Wayne of commemorative rifles by the Winchester Western Rifle people, authorized by the National Cowboy Hall of Fame. The Duke would tour the eight Dallas theaters in which *Chisum* was premiering on a tight schedule, make a small speech in each, never failing to say, "And I sure hope all you good folks never fail to vote for my good friend, Senator John Tower."

That night he had arrived at the barbeque at about the same time as the food and had moved with remarkable graciousness back and forth through the people, shaking hands, that wonderful flat face of his crinkling eternally, every wrinkle being used to extend down-home niceness to everybody.

The people trailed after him, the Texas best, saying, "Duke? John? Big John? I sure would like for you to meet . . . ," and he would say, "Nice to meet ya. . . . Nice to meet ya . . . ," and shake hands and pull a John Wayne card out of his pocket, with his autograph on the back, for whoever it was at home who needed proof that John Wayne had been met.

And more than a few of the Texas sweet little things would say, "Would you kiss me, Big John?" and he'd say,

"Sure, honey. I can do that anytime," and throw his arm around her shoulder and buss her on the cheek.

He was confronted with Daddy Billy Chisum, whose uncle actually had ridden with the original John Simpson Chisum, and John Wayne said, "You look like you got the kick in you yet of a twelve-year-old," and then looked increasingly alarmed as he realized Daddy Billy, who "still walks to town and plays checkers every day," they said, really couldn't see, couldn't hear, and didn't know why everybody was talking about someone named John Wayne and someone named John Simpson Chisum in the middle of his supper.

For two hours John Wayne had revolved like a mountain in the moonlight, doing a slow mountain dance, letting people shake his hand, being nice, making only one mistake, finally, when someone asked him, "Big John, how's your cows?" by answering, "They're fine. They're in Arizona."

Some creep from up North kept sticking a tape-recorder micro-phone in John Wayne's face with a list of questions, and Big John went right down the list with him.

"The press? They haven't done a thing that isn't wrong yet. I mean, they find the provocative so they can get more listeners and readers. It almost looks as if it is their purpose to create dissent.

"What generation gap? When I was a kid and a man came back from college with a degree at twenty-six, twenty-seven, I couldn't hardly talk with him either. They got along with a few older people and a few younger people, of course, but the rest of us couldn't make head or tail of anything he said.

"Yes, I'm concerned that my business is declining, the business of making western movies. I'm as concerned about that as I am about the fact the press, instead of creating publicity for my pictures, cre-ates nothing but dissent.

"I mean, what do you want, to throw Abbie Hoffman in against the President of the United States? That's like throwing a bantam in against Jack Dempsey, for land's sake.

"What you ought to do is point your finger at certain of the pro-fessors that teach Communism and Anarchy, and leave the kids alone.

"What do kids know?"

✦ ✦ ✦

Earlier that day, six years, seven months and two days after the assassi-nation of President John Kennedy, I had attended the dedication of the John F. Kennedy Memorial in Dallas, the city where he had been shot.

Designed by New York architect Philip Johnson, the Memorial consists of walls thirty feet high, elevated three feet off the ground, forming a fifty foot square. In the north and south walls are openings five feet wide. In the center of the roofless memorial is a black mar-ble slab, with the name, John Fitzgerald Kennedy, in gold facing north and south.

Although the idea of the Memorial had been conceived by Stanley Marcus, of the Dallas store Nieman-Marcus, the $200,000 needed for it had been raised through the contributions of 50,000 Texas citizens. Local contractors had supplied the materials free.

The dedication was mostly remarkable by who was not there.

It had been hoped that some members of the Kennedy family would come to Dallas for the dedication of the Memorial, but even in-law Stephen Smith had had to send his apologies.

President Lyndon Johnson and Governor John Connolly, both Texans, both present when John Kennedy had been shot, were not there.

There was no representative of either the state or national Democratic parties.

There was a puzzling lady present, dressed head-to-toe in black, including an impenetrable black veil, black gloves clutching a small bouquet which later she left on the Memorial.

In all, there had been no more than fifty people present at the dedication of the John F. Kennedy Memorial in Dallas.

✦ ✦ ✦

So, everybody was full of barbeque and we were standing under the adobe arch near the swimming pool with a young Pinkerton sergeant, who was going to get me out on the track next morning to let me try his Mustang with a Corvette engine, and Big John had a bottle of tequila in one hand and a glass in the other and about five in his belly, and I mentioned having attended the dedication of the John F. Kennedy Memorial.

Staring into the still, lit water of the swimming pool, John Wayne said: "I was a good friend of the Kennedys but Frank Sinatra screwed us up.

"Jack Kennedy wanted some West Coast Communist to do something and Frank called me up and said Jack wanted my advice and I said, 'That guy's a Communist and no good,' and Frank said and—believe me, I've got nothing against what's-his-name Sinatra, I like that 'Small Hotel' song he sings—and he said, 'Well, Jack has already hired him,' and I said, 'Gee whiz, then what did you ask me for? Jack wants to make the decisions the next four years, why ask me?'

"They put me in the middle that way, and I was zero with the Kennedys thereafter.

"John Kennedy was a decent man. After the Cuba thing he got some humility and then I was with him. A decent man.

"I never felt Bobby Kennedy could get the humility, you know?

"And Teddy Kennedy. There's no manliness there at all. No sense of responsibility."

And the young Pinkerton sergeant looked shocked, at me, at the pool.

And the John-Wayne symbol knew he had said something he shouldn't have said, but didn't care, after his two hundred and first movie.

He kept looking into the pool, this walking mountain of a man hesitating with his tequila, trusting me to realize, I suppose, waiting on me to see behind this indiscretion his mountain-high concern, his caring, for this country that somehow, asking him questions, Gee whiz, puts him in the middle and makes him zero with anyone who went to college or can sing the "Small Hotel" song.

John Wayne had already made the movie unique to this era: the only glamorized combat film of the war in Vietnam.

It was called *The Green Berets*, based on the novel by Robin Moore.

In making the movie, John Wayne had had the full cooperation of the United States Department of Defense.

It was in direct conflict with what the people saw of the war in Vietnam on their nightly television news.

It was a propaganda film.

It was terrible.

It turned a small profit.

6   The Car

*John Wayne's young Pinkerton sergeant was going to get me out on
the track the next morning to let me try his Mustang with a Corvette
engine.*

✦ ✦ ✦

*I'll take you ridin' in my cah-cah
The horn goes beep-beep
Engine goes brrp-brrp
Back seat, front seat
When you're ridin' in my cah . . .*
—Donovan Leitch

✦ ✦ ✦

The Los Angeles exhibition of the works of Edward Kienholz in 1966
had been delayed until March.

County officials had threatened to prevent the exhibition's opening
at all. They thought it pornographic. They had real trouble deciding
about one piece, *Rexy's*, a full-scale reproduction of two rooms in a
brothel, circa World War II.

They did not worry too much about *John Doe, The Beanery,* or
Back Seat Dodge.

John Doe: A man in a baby carriage. There is an air pipe through his
chest to the crotch of a naked woman behind him.

RIDDLE: Why is John Doe like a piano?

ANSWER: Because he is square, upright, and grand.

The Beanery: A lousy, crowded bar. All the people at the bar have clock faces. There's a woman at the end of the bar looking as tired as her fur coat. A leashed poodle sits on a bar stool. On the bar is a supper of eggs, minute steak, in grease; many beers. Loudspeakers blare the noise of competing senseless bar talk, senseless music. Even the bar-rag smell is here, almost.

Signs inside the bar read:

Capacity Three Persons—No Smoking

Minimum Service Per Person 35c

(This here 35c is for Dane to sleep.)

Faggots Stay Out

Outside The Beanery, the headline of a newspaper for sale reads: Children Kill Children in Vietnam Riots.

Back Seat Dodge: An old car, stripped, repainted an unlikely blue.

Inside, a case of Olympia beer, some bottles empty on the floor, packages of cigarettes, half empty, match papers.

The car radio is turned to a Los Angeles pop station.

Sprawled awkwardly on the cramped back seat are a boy and a girl trying to make love, maybe making it. Only their shoes and socks are on.

The boy is made of chicken wire.

✦ ✦ ✦

A somber, stately morning procession of cars came down the wide washboard road from the highway to the track, weirdly painted cars, some new, some old, some unlike anything usually seen, silver, red, black, yellow, striped, stripped, oddly low, oddly high, jutting fronts, jutting backs, wheels big, small, fat, narrow.

Some came on platform trailers behind station wagons: dragsters in long, enclosed, highly decorated cases; motorcycles held upright, steady by guy wires, exactly in the middle of their trailers, sculptured pieces in steel and grease.

As they turned right into the pits before the track the signs painted on the car bodies could be read: King Chevy Olds, Robie Ford, Miss Smylie Buick, Cutler Ford, Foss Motors, Harris Sales (lettering and art by Mo).

In the pits, the kids-men who are racing this week, in cheap clothes, work boots, white socks, pants narrow for riding, open sport shirts, sweaters, hair combed the old way, with oil, have whiter faces, garage faces, serious eyes, muddier boots, overalls, the flat expressions of self-conscious people, not twitching, constantly adjusting their shoulders. They seldom spoke to each other through the fumes, the incredible noise of constantly gunned engines.

Girl friends, wives (chicks, old ladies), were to race against each other in powder puffs, Corvettes, Impalas, in the Debutante Derby, sitting straight behind their steering wheels, hands at eleven and one on a clockface, in good tweed slacks, freshly done hair.

There are bikes, stock cars, dragsters. "Tuned in the Village by the Little People." All Sunday morning the cloud of exhaust builds over the pits as mufflers are by-passed and three hundred and fifty cars are given their final tuning.

At least four thousand dollars was needed to prepare a car for racing, plus at least fifty dollars a day to race, for plugs, points, gas, tow, tires.

The prize for a Class Win at most big tracks was fifty dollars, plus a trophy.

Mostly the racers worked in garages as mechanics, long hours, for the money, the time, the place to work, the tools.

By noon, almost five thousand people are in the stands across the tracks from the pits, and the dry, acrid smell of the exhaust clouds up to them, the flatulent explosions of too many cars together without mufflers, more constant, louder, than the roar of all the football crowds in history cheering every score ever made.

The American flag is always raised before the races start.

Once, when the public address system was broken, the flag was raised silently, without the usual playing of the national anthem.

Seeing the flag rise, the people in the stands stood up anyway.

It used to be with horses in these same pastures. Kids, usually without saddles, trying horses against each other two-by-two for the quarter-mile in the autumn dusk, after school, between chores and homework, blue jeans and checkered shirts, horses surprised to find themselves racing, feeling the sheer joy of it themselves, disappearing down the field toward the line of trees.

Then it was with cars, in these same pastures, only usually at night, because there was something more sinister about cars. The cops had something to say about them and how we used them.

We would line up the respectable cars, family cars borrowed for the evening "to go to the library just for a minute," in two lanes, spaced, facing each other, beams on low to light the quarter-mile distance without blinding the kids across the track, and we would race two pre-Wars, Chevies or Fords kids had worked on, sort of, against each other, rear wheels spinning on cow flops, wet grass, cars bouncing, swerving over the pasture, making girls squeal. Kids would sit on fenders along the two lanes above their headlights, to see, and they would be able to move quickly to the rear of their cars, if one of the drivers coming down the field should lose control.

Sometimes we would race the same quarter-mile backwards, left hand on the open, swaying door, right hand on the wheel, head craned out the door to see where we were going down the alley of double lights.

We were terribly committed to Ford or Chevy, huge American companies we were able to feel personal about at fourteen, fifteen, sixteen, as if it mattered, as if it could ever matter.

The whole quarter-mile thing is American, youth: that there is virtue in the fast start, the short burst; that speed itself is full of promise, although sustaining it beyond two thousand feet is hopeless, impossible, unimportant anyway. Everything is spent on beginnings, as if beginnings themselves have separate, intense meaning.

In the mid-1960s there were more than three hundred official, that is, known, sanctioned, admitted-to dragstrips in the United States.

In 1958, a professor of physics, who will remain nameless here, said it was impossible for a wheel-driven car to go over 167 miles per hour, within a quarter-mile.

In the mid-1960s, the record stood at 222 miles per hour.

Black-leather spidermen, prone on their macho-machines, legs straddling engines gunning, gunning, waiting for the lights.

Six timed yellow lights in a vertical bank signal sign ripple down to a final green.

Bikes bolt, front tires slapping the tar once, hard. Legs retract, bodies elongate, feet prop near the axle of the rear wheel, helmeted heads jut forward of the straight, twenty-inch handlebars, knees bent slightly, an inch or less above the pavement, genitals bearing almost the entire racer's weight on the merciless, vibrating seat, a piece of leather with less padding than a first baseman's mitt.

The thing, man and motorcycle, bullet up the slight incline, eastward, away from the afternoon sun. Shoulders heave in exhalation with each shift of gears. Beyond the second shift the front wheel might come off the tar again, slam it; the racer's flat body inches forward on the machine to bring the weight off the rear.

The age-old temptation to turn the head, look over the shoulder at the motorcycle in the other lane is given in to, time and again.

"Look at them go, folks. Two young men in a great hurry. Mike has worked hard on that bike: two engines on one bike, developing over one hundred cubic inches of impact. Really burns up the pavement."

Two-by-two stock cars come to the line, engines so overpowered they can't go forward slowly without jerking, placing themselves at a slight angle to the line so one wheel stops the radar light. The other wheel is actually a little forward of the light.

Air intakes, organ pipes through the dashboard, one for each cylinder. The driver looks huge on the seat in back.

The engines gun. Behind the cars clouds of exhaust conceal other, cars waiting on the ramp. Fat tires grind slowly in place, prance.

The lights ripple to green, the cars break free with a screech, a roar, maybe a lurch sideways, as the power behind it is really too much, a barely perceptible pause at the first shift, five or six feet from the starting line, swerve a little down the lane, the front end planing slightly for the last meters, across the line down the tracks, coasting then, the silence of these engines with the gas off sudden, complete, as they slow to turning speed.

"One hundred and twenty-three miles an hour . . . how would you like to leave them standing at a streetlight with that? And a very nice paint job, too, Frank. We've got two dragsters coming up, ladies and gentlemen, after this race. Butch is going to run his chariot against Jack Doyle again."

A kid in a black leather jacket astride a bike on a trailer being hauled down the service lane behind his parents' car watches the race coolly, like a young Caesar entering Rome after a successful campaign, a hero now detached, but willing to be interested.

From the pits now dragsters are pushed onto the middle of the track from a separate ramp by a truck or station wagon, bursting into sound as they are rolled toward the control tower, go beyond it by themselves, turn, their front bike-wheels actually laying over as they turn, their sixteen foot rods seeming terribly long leading into the custom-fitting, chariot cockpit, the racer huddled in a shiny suit, helmet, thick gloves, face mask, goggles, trying to stay out of the heat of his own exhausts, toeing the line, revealing parachute pouches prim in back, little purses carried by brute machinery, real rods which jump at the green light like Thoroughbreds.

The drivers lean forward in the blast of heat, having to lean back, fight the wheel with straight arms, up the track in a roar of power, a bang of engines slammed into gear, a bomb-cloud of exhaust and burning rubber fragments, keeping the trotter-light, leaping front-end down.

Beyond the finish line, the parachutes trail out and twirl prettily, counterclockwise, against the background of dark woods.

Down the service lane pours a noisy cortege of people who have raced, bikes nosed by cars, factories, powder puffs, dragsters pushed by woodies, even a Caddie flower car, back to the control tower where they are handed their trophies or time cards through a back window, sometimes stopping again beyond the window, to pick up the wife and kids, or husband, before returning to the pits.

"What did you get, twelve-six?"

A solemn nod, a shrug: "Twelve-six."

Driving home on highways in the Saturday twilights, trailers bearing motorcycles, powder puffs, hot rods and dragsters being pulled by the family cars, these contestants for speed, the champions and the losers, would be in heavy traffic all the way, bumper-to-bumper.

✦ ✦ ✦

I can drive, but I've never had a license. I can drive on the highway, but not downtown. All my friends are the best drivers. Neal driving me three thousand miles across the country, all the time looking me in the eyes.

I'm afraid of cars, I'm not afraid of horses. Horses can fight back. Cars might hit somebody.

—Jack Kerouac, author of *On the Road*

7 The Seeds of Revolution

Over lunch, film director Otto Preminger said, "I, too, am against violence. But I partly feel the generation gap is the fault of the older people. They will not listen. All the kids want is to be listened to. "Nobody likes the police, in history. You call police on people and they resent it and they will fight.

"The war, civil rights; it is very regrettable there are riots. But in history . . . we treasure our freedom, our independence. But we did not get them without riots.

"Because unfortunately people are greedy. They do not give up what they have.

"And one can be hungry only so long without getting mad. Being violent."

✦ ✦ ✦

"I am in this country just now to be useful," said Ralph Schoenman. "If I could be more useful somewhere else, I would be there."

We sat in leather chairs in a small, quiet, book-lined room not far from where Schoenman shortly was to speak to the undergraduates at Tufts University.

Ralph Schoenman had been described to me as secretary to the English mathematician and philosopher, antiwar and anti-nuclear weapons activist, Lord Bertrand Russell.

We met shortly after the conclusion of the fourth War Crimes Tribunal. The first two sessions, not open to the public, had been held in three places, Hanoi, Tokyo and London, in 1966.

The two public sessions, held in Stockholm in May and Copenhagen in November 1967, considered five questions: had the United States committed aggression in Vietnam; bombed civilian populations; used experimental weapons; tortured and mutilated prisoners; committed genocide in South Vietnam by "placing fifty-nine percent of South Vietnam's population in concentration camps"?

Asked precisely the authorship of the War Crimes Tribunal, Schoenman answered, "I wouldn't claim authorship of the War Crimes Tribunal. I had an important part in its formulation, but Russell inaugurated it."

At that time, Lord Russell was ninety-five years old; Schoenman thirty-two. Schoenman had produced a book on Lord Russell, *Philosopher of the Century,* which Little Brown had published in January 1968.

A man saturnine in appearance, beard-line precisely reciprocal with his hairline, eyebrows which V'd easily over small, deep brown eyes, Schoenman affected a proletarian blue sweater under a worker's Sunday black suit. Talking to students, even casually, he would remove his coat, leaving him in the collegiately bulky sweater. His hands, usually fingering a short cigar, were ironically dirty, considering their softness.

I found him uncommonly frank on his own past, and interesting on the topic of how seeds of revolution can be sown from the top.

All according to Schoenman, at age fifteen Schoenman's father found it necessary to leave Hungary after the collapse of the Hungarian Communist revolution in 1918. The father came west, to the United States, settling originally in New York and then California, rather than going east to Russia, where the Communist revolution had been more successful, because "he felt it more his duty to promulgate communism in countries where it was unknown, than to luxuriate in the Soviet."

In the United States, the elder Schoenman became the owner of what his son described as "a one-man paint factory," and sent his son to Princeton.

Ralph spent his junior Princeton year "salmon fishing from an Alaskan port, off the coast of Russia." He was not in academic difficulty. His concentration was philosophy; his honors thesis on the social-revolutionary ideas of Plato. In our immediately subsequent conversation, in an effort to find common ground, I used a few nautical terms. Schoenman did not respond to these terms with any understanding. I think it safe to report, that Ralph Schoenman spent his junior year at Princeton off-shore.

His application for a United States passport that year, 1956 (Ralph Schoenman was Princeton class of 1958), was rejected by the State Department. It took two years and a decision by the United States Supreme Court before Schoenman was granted a passport.

After graduating Princeton, Schoenman won a master of science degree at the London School of Economics.

In England, Schoenman became a member of the Executive Youth Board of the Nuclear Disarmament Committee. The aims of the committee were to end American occupation of military bases in Great Britain, and to get Britain out of the North Atlantic Treaty Organization.

Lord Russell was president of the Nuclear Disarmament Committee.

Schoenman wrote Lord Russell a personal letter advocating a more militant stand. In response, Lord Russell invited Schoenman to his country home in Penrhyndeudraeth, North Wales. That was in early 1960. During his visit, Schoenman suggested to the earl making the Nuclear Disarmament Committee more effective by: 1) developing mass civil disobedience against nuclear weapons, military bases and NATO, and 2) involving the working class more in the struggle.

Sitting small in his chair, speaking in a teacherly manner, Schoenman said: "We agreed we had to advance our campaign by using more militant forms. And Russell said he would like to be involved in that. I said I would canvass people about their ideas as to how to do this.

"I came up with a form-letter scheme. We gave five forms to one individual and he was to send them out to five other individuals. In that way we were able to reach three thousand people within five stages, each person knowing only the person who contacted him. Therefore, it was sort of cellular.

"We decided we would do nothing without a minimum of two thousand people. This gave people a great sense of security. We were able to say to them, if you come out to demonstrate we guarantee you there will be at least two thousand people there, or no demonstration. The cops could not arrest two thousand people.

"Shortly, people in Bristol were getting letters and asking who we were. We realized that first we had to win people."

Schoenman resolved this public relations problem by asking Lord Russell to approach prominent people personally, such as sculptor Henry Moore and playwright Robert Bolt, and ask them to join a Committee of 100, which committee would actively and publicly practice civil disobedience.

"In other words," Schoenman explained, "we alienated the intellectual community from government policy. What could the government do? Denounce its one hundred most prominent citizens?

"What we did then was to radicalize this group. In our first demonstration, at the Ministry of Defense, six thousand sat down and ten thousand marched. The police ordered the firemen to spray their fire hoses on the crowd, and the firemen refused.

"The movement grew rapidly and the government became scared. Before our third demonstration, at Parliament Square, the government developed panic. It announced that anyone found within a mile radius of the square, up to twenty-four hours before the scheduled demonstration, whether a demonstrator or not, was liable to be arrested and imprisoned for up to six months.

"Nearly eighty thousand people showed up. The police were vicious. They made the mistake of rupturing the kidneys of a cousin of the Home Secretary."

As a result of this demonstration in Parliament Square, Lord Russell and his wife, thirty years his junior, were imprisoned for seven days. Schoenman was imprisoned for two months.

According to Schoenman, the demonstration in Parliament Square was the peak of the movement, and the moment the movement failed.

"When we were arrested, the youngsters who took over the movement were confronted with enthusiasm. Bloated by success, they planned simultaneous demonstrations in Edinburgh, Bristol, Manchester and Coventry, and proposed to surround and occupy a Strategic Air Command base near Oxford, the nuclear base at Weathersfield, and the York Bomber Command—all on the same day, seven weeks hence. Thirteen 'committees of 100' sprang up overnight.

"So you can understand what happened. They jumped from a single demonstration to an assualt on the military technology of the Western World.

"The government invoked the Official Secrets Act, which meant demonstrators were facing not six months but fourteen years in jail."

"Lord Russell," I commented, "was released from prison early enough to stop this exuberant plan."

"Yes."

"But you were not."

"That's right."

"And the plan went forward."

"Yes."

The demonstrations that day drew only ten thousand people. The six members of the Committees of one hundred who were arrested received jail sentences of eighteen months each.

Schoenman said, "From that moment, the Antiwar Movement in Britain went into a rapid decline. There was a loss of confidence in the leadership. We could never mobilize the same forces again."

Schoenman's secretaryship to Lord Russell became formalized in 1961, when Schoenman was in prison, only to obstruct a government move to deport him from England.

As Lord Russell's secretary, a position Schoenman stated gave him "almost diplomatic immunity," Schoenman travelled to sixty-two countries over the next five years. He held discussions with over twenty heads of state, including Chou En-lai, Nasser, Ben Bella, Ho Chi Minh, Pham Van Dong, Fidel Castro and "various other leaders of revolutionary movements." He attended most international Communist meetings, on both sides of the iron curtain, and spent prolonged periods both in the Soviet Union and Communist China.

He said his activities during those five years were financed by the Russell Foundation, and "other angels, including the Communist parties indigenous to the countries I have visited."

Before being asked, Schoenman repeated and denied the charge that he "manipulated Lord Russell."

"I travel between seventy-five and eighty percent of the time. I have for five years. Russell is continuously exposed to journalists. It's flattering but fatuous to think that a man involved in the anti-imperialist struggle since the Boer War should need a youngster to give him political orientation."

A cornerstone of Bertrand Russell's philosophy is that Man does not directly perceive an independent world of fact, but only a continuum of his own belief-influenced perceptions. Where the internal world of belief and the external world of fact correspond is truth.

Again by personal contact, according to Schoenman, Russell persuaded an impressive list of international household names, with intellectual or revolutionary credentials, to join him in the War Crimes Tribunals. The purpose was to hear evidence that United States' role in Vietnam was criminal. President of the Tribunal was Jean-Paul Sartre. Americans on the Tribunal included Stokely Carmichael, David Dellinger and James Baldwin.

Evidence was given orally by American ex-soldiers. Documentary films by North Vietnamese and Japanese film crews, and by French cameraman Roger Pic were viewed.

The films the Tribunal saw showed airplanes with American markings dropping bombs that burst into rapidly spreading fire upon impact in jungles, on dams and dikes, in villages and towns. Other films showed men in American uniforms beating and kicking bound prisoners, pressing knives into prisoners' throats, and slitting open a prisoner's stomach. Scenes were shown of Nam Dinh, once North Vietnam's third largest city, population ninety thousand, bombed out of existence by fifty-four bombing raids between June 1965 and December 1966.

"The Tribunal asked President Lyndon Johnson and Secretary of State Dean Rusk to either appear or cause to have evidence presented," Schoenman said.

Dean Rusk answered: "I do not play games with senile old men."

The conclusions of the Tribunals were precisely in accord with its original indictments.

Instead of attending the fourth War Crimes Tribunal session, Schoenman spent four months in Bolivia, as "part of a committee sent by Russell to investigate the trial of Regis Debray."

Debray, to whom Schoenman referred as "one of the great revolutionaries," was captured and tried by the Bolivian government after he had held conversations with Cuban revolutionary, Ernesto "Che" Guevara in interior Bolivia. Debray had some credentials as a French journalist.

"During the end of the trial," Schoenman stated, "I submitted an offer of proof to the military tribunal. It proved that Regis had been tortured. Witnesses murdered. I called for the nullification of the trial.

"This, of course, led to my own arrest, detention for a week, and expulsion from the country."

In his proof, Schoenman mentioned one Jorge Vasquez in particular, "who," he said, "could have given valuable evidence at the trial, but instead had his four limbs broken, chest opened, and was killed . . ." before he could testify.

During the trial of Regis Debray, Che Guevara was found by Bolivian soldiers and killed.

✦ ✦ ✦

Schoenman's lecture to the students, entitled "The World in Revolution," lasted precisely forty-two minutes.

Standing behind the podium in his bulky sweater, Schoenman told the university students:

> Southeast Asia provides ninety percent of the world's crude rubber, sixty percent of its tin. . . . America has attacked Vietnam because it wants its natural resources. . . . The Capitol Building could be swallowed by any one of the five segments of the Pentagon. . . . The Pentagon is directly related to large-scale capitalism in the United States. Subcontracts awarded by the United States are in every major city of the country. . . . And what is the secret army? The Central Intelligence Agency . . . seventy-five percent of its budget is spent within the United States, purchasing universities, and magazines. . . . The system is violent, the struggle which is sweeping the world is violent . . . the chickens are coming home to roost. . . . And I suggest to you, living in the belly of the beast, the choice is narrow.

There was a question and answer period, during which Ralph Schoenman's face became increasingly red.

Q: What are the strategic prospects for armed uprising in the belly of the beast?
A: The black uprising is the harbinger in this country of the second American Revolution.

Q: Won't the American working class form a counterrevolution?
A: It is a mistake to underestimate the root experience of the white middle class.

Q: How important is war to our present economy?

A: The system needs war like a drug addict needs a fix.

Q: If it is the duty of a revolutionary to make revolution, isn't it also the duty of an imperialist to maintain imperialism?

A: To just play word games isn't worthy.

Upon entering the United States, after his various adventures abroad, Ralph Schoenman had his passport picked up by authorities. Shortly, he left the United States, without his passport.

8   Dolls

If it is the duty of a revolutionary to make revolution, isn't it also the duty of an imperialist to maintain imperialism?

—A student at Tufts University

✦ ✦ ✦

Anthropologists! Consider Gretchen, the inflatable lifesized doll! No assembly is necessary! Just add air to her flesh-tone, lifelike vinyl body and *presto!* you have a five-foot-four beauty . . .

Offered in the spring of 1969 by Frankfurt Imports, Sepulveda, California, Gretchen's movable, soft, lifelike body can be dressed in the popular size nine clothes of a glamor girl! A different, fun item to dress up your office, and become the conversation piece of your clients! Be the talk of the neighborhood with this "girl" at poolside! (She even floats!) Set by a window, she will be somebody at home when burglars are casing the neighborhood!

What better status symbol could you find at the price? (Nine dollars and ninety-five cents.)

A deluxe model of Gretchen (complete with wig and bikini!) is available for sixteen dollars and ninety-five cents.

✦ ✦ ✦

In 1968, American poet Rod McKuen's personal income was reported to be 3.5 million dollars.

✦ ✦ ✦

I spent an afternoon sneaking up on Tiny Tim.

Tiny Tim!

Autographing Record Albums! the department store newspaper advertisement said. From Three-thirty to Five o'clock!

At three-thirty there were two eight-year-old girls outside the department store singing in falsetto, giggling, and saying, "Oooo! I'm Tiny Tim! Yuck!"

Inside the department store at three-thirty over three hundred people waited in a long, wiggly line. Some were over fourteen years old.

Lo, at a desk in a comer between records and books, nose and teeth draped by hair, sat the timorous singing star, signing autographs on slips of paper, not record albums, for kids who had stood in line in that same department store to climb onto Santa's knee not many years before.

Over Tiny Tim's head was an orange and white sign saying Camping Corner.

With the help of a tape recording playing somewhere, Tiny Tim's tremorous "I Love You Truly" seemed to tipnose through his two lips.

"Why are you standing in line?" I asked a woman.

"For my daughter," she said, smiling fondly at a fierce-looking nine-year-old under her hands.

Ten minutes later I returned and asked the daughter, "Why are you standing in line?"

"For my mother," she said sourly.

Someone who went through the line told me Tiny Tim made a tiny check mark on a tiny pad of paper under his elbow every time he saw a kid in line who had actually bought an album of his.

There was one man in line with a weathered face, a work jacket, fedora hat. I could not figure what he was doing there.

But the expression on his face said he would brain anyone who asked.

Outside the line, leaning against a counter, sweatered arms akimbo, lounged the fifteen-year-old boy clearly for whom all this had been arranged. Young girls were parading by him at about the rate of fifteen a minute. His cool eyes inspected each one, undressed them, tousled their hair, did whatever else, I suppose dressed them again, and put them back in line.

It was a temptation to ask for the autograph of such an enterprising young man.

✦ ✦ ✦

Rock star Jimi Hendrix sat on the sill of the front door of the house he had just bought in London's Mayfair district.

A blue plaque on the door said the house once had been inhabited by Georg Friedrich Handel.

Chin on hands, eyes studying his wriggling naked toes, Hendrix said, "I didn't know this was Handel's pad, man, until after I got in.

"Tell the truth, I haven't heard much of the fella's stuff. But I dig a bit of Bach now and again. . . ."

9 Did Andy Warhol Spoil Success for Rock Hudson?

We went to an Andy Warhol party and interviewed ourselves in his reflecting glasses.

Andy Warhol first established his vanishing presence in 1957–8. His art was existential, intensified the immediate by denying the past, denying the future, by choosing and perceiving the essence of only the most transitory. He was lionized.

Some lionized him because they understood him.

Others lionized him because they thought him a delightful fraud, a self-made gimmick in an age which happily responded to such, an appearance utterly departed from reality in a society which inclined to put appearance well ahead of reality, a complete negative in a world fresh out of positives. Like a little candle in a cavernous church, his existence was only noticed because he flickered.

If contemporary heroism was the achievement of success without the fact of work, Warhol was a Napoleon. He was a tower of passivity.

In his Factory, a New York City silver-lined loft, his works were assembled for him by his gnomes. Static works, movies, helium-filled pillows he sold as clouds were put together under his direction but seldom with his direct involvement. Occasionally he languished a brush, or stood by a camera, but even this effort was soon resisted altogether, as too sapping of his energies.

He insisted, in the fall of 1966, he would do no more painting. His underground movies required his full attention. The nightclub he owned jointly with Bob Dylan, the Velvet Underground, was the prime source of his lack of amusement.

Cars and a shooting: even in the life of a one hundred–pound artist.

Before Warhol arrived at his own party, we toured his works.

One Hundred Campbell Soup Cans, 1962, acrylic on canvas (Beef Noodle), *Three Campbell Soup Cans*, acrylic and silk screen enamel on canvas (Condensed), his *Twenty-Four Brillo Boxes*, his works of atrocity, *Saturday Disaster*, 1964 (duplicate photos of an auto accident, one body hanging from the roof, another spilling from the seat to the ground), *Electric Chair*, 1964, in shocking red and yellow and grey and white, *Orange Disaster #5* (fifteen sombre electric chairs with shocking yellow backgrounds); grossly overstated flower designs (red and yellow on jungle green background). There were two portraits, one of a pretty girl, which did not flatter the subject, *Holly Solomon*, in nine identical panels, and *Self-Portrait*, which did, in twenty-four identical panels.

On two consoles, three of Warhol's ideas of what a movie should be reeled endlessly. *Eat* portrayed a man biting and chewing a mushroom but never seeming to get anywhere with it. *Kiss* showed, close up, a couple osculating long beyond what human patience ordinarily permits. The third, *Sleep*, was far more osculant with viewer reaction.

Perhaps the most original piece was *Do It Yourself*, 1962, acrylic on canvas, a seascape, blue sky and pink clouds painted in, a pencil outline of two yachts, both schooners, the rest a sea of numbers, à la number painting.

As is proper for someone being lionized, there was a rush for Andy Warhol when he entered the party, the hero of minimalism and multiplicity, who had made such a vast presence out of disappearance, who had made some oft-quoted crack as "Sooner or later, everyone will be a celebrity for twenty minutes."

Extremely small—"He's always on some diet or other," reported a companion, David Whitney; "wispy is the word"—his hair was silvered with a drugstore dye, his drawn face made up with a fairly thick paste, and his eyes were hidden behind one-way, silver-fronted sunglasses, never removed in public. His thin hands, his wrists denied the need for makeup, deathly frail, pastey white. (Two years after first meeting Warhol, I was told by James Klee, then an assistant professor of psychology at Brandeis University, that Andy Warhol was piebald. Curiously, Klee had had both Andy Warhol and Abbie Hoffman as students. According to Klee, as a student Warhol was painfully self-conscious of his abnormalcy.) He hovered in the shadows of a room; one had to look to see him, train one's eyes to distinguish him from the cracks in the floor. When forced, he came forward to meet one in an apparent fainting condition on wobbly knees; he spoke in a whisper more or less to a single ear.

His touted entourage looked like a group of children tumbling back downstairs after having been sent to spend a rainy afternoon playing among the wardrobes in the attics. One wore an old, wide-lapel tuxedo, white open shirt and, of course, sneakers. Another's suit was of silver-threaded upholstery fabric. The most constant waiting lady, International Velvet (Warhol resists the suggestion her alias is designed to one-up a fictional race horse once nuzzled by Elizabeth Taylor; the rumor passed through the party that she was a Bottomley, which caused newspapeman/sailor Phillip Weld to enquire if she was, one of the horse-Bottomleys), carried copies of *Vogue* and *Bazaar* against her chest but dressed in the hooded capes and black, baseball-sized, dangling earrings previously featured only in the cartoons of Charles Addams. From dust, they were.

In June 1969, one of his entourage, Valerie Solanos, the "antimale star" of *I, a Man*, was to be sentenced to three years in jail for shooting Andy Warhol. It was a remarkable feat, probably the most extraordinary example of marksmanship in the history of womankind.

Warhol's personal integrity was symbolized by his all-occasion brown leather jacket, dirty white shirt, black trousers, which would have been tight on anyone less emaciated, but on him sagged and bagged, held up by a wide silver belt, the weightiest thing about him.

Warhol's covering almost everything with silver, including himself, expresses his solid interest in the ephemeral. That which is present, yet almost does not exist, approaches essence. He likes silver, he said, because, due to its odd surface qualities, "it makes things disappear."

"My work has no future at all. I know that. A few years. Of course my images will mean nothing."

"Does your lack of posterity bother you?"

"No."

"If you agree your work has no posterity, is it art?"

"Yes."

"You say there can be an art without a posterity?"

"Yes."

A conscious celebration of the immediate.

Has there been an age so surrounded by the transitory, the impermanent? To our forebears, a tomato was recognizable as a tomato because it had the properties of a tomato. To us, a tomato is recognizable as a tomato by the label on the tomato can, which will change. Is a rose a rose?

His static work made this point. By offering to the viewer the commonplace in duplicate he celebrated, made conscious, the immediate experience of seeing the transitory love goddess, news photo, commercial package. These common things, so present in our existence, achieve an almost essential nonexistence; their presence cannot extend beyond the immediate; their multiple existence, without a past, without a future, makes them existentially precious things. No matter how many times the image of the Coke bottle is repeated today, its identity cannot extend into tomorrow.

This is the essence of modern existence. The ratio of the impermanent to the permanent may be the reverse of what we have known in history.

The man eats his mushroom, but nothing is consumed; the couple kiss, but nothing is consummated; even sleep does not extend beyond the now.

Today we presume accelerating change. The cigarette package, as constantly in our hands as prayer beads in the hands of a monk, will be replaced next year by a newer design. The change in our neighborhoods is noticeable after a summer's vacation. Few can go back to his old school and find it as it was, or frequently even where it was. Today's newspaper exists in six hundred thousand copies; what will be the level of existence of today's newspaper tomorrow? The television report of the end of the world will be contained in a ninety second segment.

The more transitory things are, the more meaningless. Reality, our environment, our existence, is cluttered by things deprived of meaning by their sheer impermanence. The most immediate has no past, and no future: simple, lateral multiplicity. Of more meaning, then, is transition itself. Essence of immediacy is gained by that which is most denied permanence.

Warhol's work, by itself, is without a future, he says. His success has been in intensifying the immediate by denying the past, denying the future, by choosing and perceiving the essence of only the most transitory.

But his vision probably is permanent. If the presumption of accelerating change is accurate, after Warhol there will come other artists to celebrate with us, make conscious and intense, those things of our immediate world, including ourselves, which have only the most limited existence.

✦ ✦ ✦

Lunching at Aunt Pittypat's Porch, in Atlanta, Georgia, film star Rock Hudson told me the following story on himself:

"When I was twenty-two or twenty-three I went on my first publicity trip: Portland, Oregon.

"There was a big parade through town. Bands. We each had our own convertible with our names plastered on the sides.

"When we got to the theater, police had made a corridor through the crowd, their arms locked Indian fashion. When I was halfway across the sidewalk the crowds squeezed in, banging the policemen's heads together, and I had to hit the sidewalk and crawl on my hands and knees into the theater.

"I didn't sleep a wink that night. I was too excited. I had really liked that. I decided I would like some more of it.

"So the next day I walked along the parade route all by myself, hoping to be mauled. No one recognized me. Store windows had my pictures in them. I stood beside one for a long time and no one even smiled at me. I was really crushed.

"I didn't sleep, that night, either. I decided I had learned my lesson."

10   Hugh MacDiarmid

*What you ought to do is point your finger at certain of the professors
that teach Communism and Anarchy, and leave the kids alone.*

—John Wayne

✦ ✦ ✦

At eleven-fifteen they were just finishing breakfast in the dining room
with black coffee and quick trips to the kitchen.

"Well," said Hugh MacDiarmid himself. "You don't look any better than we do. Were you with us last night?"

"We were up rather late," said his friend from home, MacCaig.
"Celebrating we're not sure what."

There he was, an old-looking seventy-four, getting up, leaning on
the table, the "wee little mon," the scourge of the world in a kilt,
Murray of Tullibardine plaid ("Red suits me better, you know, the
fiery temperament"), little green Scottish jacket, no pockets, of
course, pale green tie, long white hair and moustache. His eyes were
so close together I thought I was looking straight down a pair of open
scissors. But the wonderful thing no one could have thought, put on
him, even to jig in the imagination, were his beautiful blue sneakers,
plimsolls, not a wrinkle in them.

In 1967 the American Macmillan publishing company produced
The Collected Poems of Hugh MacDiarmid, from *Annals of the Five
Senses* (1923) to a *A Drunk Man Looks at the Thistle* (1926; 88 pages

long: what a drunk, what a thistle!) to the very last, *The Caledonian Antisyzygy*, part of the hitherto uncollected. "They excerpted me," he said. "They're excerpted, you know."

A speaking tour of American campuses was arranged, but then the State Department refused MacDiarmid a visa, and the lectures had to be postponed.

In Scotland, MacDiarmid had always been in complete, collected, unexpurgated trouble.

The Communist Party kept throwing him out because he declared himself a Nationalist every other Thursday.

The Nationalists wouldn't have him because of his Communist leanings.

What he was trying to do was to get the international Communist movement to support the Scottish National movement.

He wanted Scotland free of England.

The result was that he was accredited with originating the idea that the international Communist movement should support national liberation fronts generally. Such as the Viet Cong.

For reasons unknown (the protests of poetry lovers?) the State Department suddenly reversed itself. A visa was granted with a precise stipulation, clearly understood by MacDiarmid.

He would come speak at American campuses, as long as he said nothing political.

And even poetry lovers in Scotland, who said Hugh MacDiarmid was the greatest poet alive, were known to have become fretful when MacDiarmid was found taking some lines from a novel and standing them up in verse and declaring them his own poem.

"My way of complimenting the author," he said.

His tour, when it began, was so sudden and quick that I found myself spending most of the night dashing cross-country to have breakfast with him in the home of a professor at the first college on tour. I was eager to meet a poet who had caused all that trouble. Our meeting was to be shrouded in secrecy. It was known he was being followed and tape-recorded by the Federal Bureau of Investigation.

Driving the final distance at that hour of the day I created the "turrible mon" in my windshield, a wee little man in a kilt and knee socks, Scottish jacket and tam, the Scottish face of a demon, eyes deep in wet sand.

> I maun feed frae the common trough ana'
> Whaur a' the lees o' hope are jumbled up;
> While centuries like pigs are slorpin' owre't.

> (I must feed from the common trough as well
> Where all the dregs of hope are jumbled up;
> While centuries like pigs are slurping over it).

"He has done more for English poetry by committing some of his finest verse to Scots than if he had elected to write exclusively in the Southern dialect," said T. S. Eliot.

> In wi' your gruntle then, puir wheegin' saul,
> Lap up the ugsome aidle wi' the lave,
> What gin it's your ain vomit that you swill.

> (In with your snout then, poor whinin' soul,
> Lap up the ugly slop with the rest,
> What if it's your own vomit that you swill).

And then there are his lines:

> The spirit of Man
> Is a bird in a cage,
> That beats on the bars
> Wi' a goodly rage.

"What do you think of seven dollars and ninety-five cents for the price of your book?" I asked him.

"You'll have to shout," said MacCaig. "He's as deaf as a board."

"Ochone, it's awful," said himself. "I'd have to save half my life to pay it."

"More than twice that, Christopher, for you," said MacCaig.

"Would you like some coffee and . . . ?" asked MacDiarmid. "We almost waited."

"Tell me," I said, while we settled back around the dining table, cottage style. "Why the pen name?"

"Well, you see, I was born too close to the border," said Christopher Murray (Hugh MacDiarmid) Grieve. "I was almost English."

"Heaven forbid."

"It did, you see. I thought Hugh MacDiarmid would be more representative of all the Scots."

"Even the sober ones," said MacCaig.

According to MacCaig, MacDiarmid lived twenty-five miles from Edinburgh.

"Do I? That far? I get in quite often."

MacCaig said, "Aye, and when he does, it's a disaster."

"A what?"

"A disaster, Christopher."

"It is not."

"Believe me," said MacCaig. "It's a disaster. I'm the one who knows."

"It may be," said MacDiarmid. "At that."

I asked what he'd been talking about to students, the twice he'd been let see them.

"The weather," said MacCaig. "He's commented on the weather in Edinburgh quite extensively."

"I'm grateful to your state department," said MacDiarmid, beginning to make one of those statements which always go awry and is misquoted. "They gave me a narrow visa and weren't happy to let me in at all. I didn't believe I presented any genuine danger to the United States. My ingenuous appearance dissuaded them."

"His bonny bloodshot eyes dissuaded them," said MacCaig.

"I regret my visit to this country, my first and probably my last, is so short. There are so many people and things in this country that interest me."

"Talk of the weather, Christopher."

"But I'm grateful they let me in at all."

"They didn't even give him a rest day," said MacCaig. "On the visa. He has to go the last day he speaks."

"What's this about your being a Communist?" I asked.

"I'm a Communist."

"He's the world's most complacent and courteous revolutionary," said MacCaig.

"Does your being a Communist get in the way of your being a Nationalist?"

"Ah, don't you see?" Although he was playing with a stubby pipe, he was smoking Lucky Strike. "The party's come around to my way of thinking. They realize now, after forty years of my telling them, that their strength is in the national liberation fronts."

"The weather, Christopher. It's a nice day in Edinburgh, no doot."

"What? You know, no Scot with a sense would drink blended whiskey if he could get a malt."

"We can't get a malt here?"

"We're canny," said MacDiarmid. "We keep it at home."

MacCaig said, "He drank it all before he left, he did."

"Of course, I'm not prejudiced against anything alcoholic, you know. I'm liberal that way, too."

"What will be the result of your liberal ferment?" I asked.

"The freedom of Scotland," he said. "I'll live to see it."

"You won't make it to lunch, Christopher."

"In ten years. And I'll make it. I've spent my life squandering the model health of my forebears. Oooo, they were model. I've got a good ten years."

"About the poetry," I said. "Don't the politics get in the way of the poetry?"

"There's nothing wrong with good propaganda," said he, "as long as it's in a good poem."

I noted that his poems over the years came away from the Scots dialect.

"Well, I said to myself years ago that to be in tune, to use science, I must detour away from the dialect. I mean to get back to Scots, one day. I think I can carry Scots a great deal further than I have."

I understood there were to be three phases of his poetry before he was through, before Scotland was free, before he had squandered all his forebears' model health. The first, of Scottish songs; the second, of poems in English, Southern dialect, which got him used to modern words, scientific terms; the third, which he was then not far into, using modern scientific terms in forms, sounds, closer to Scots songs.

"Speaking of a' that," he said. "The flexibility of my poetry is a result of my nondogmatic political position."

"Tell him a good malt whiskey," said MacCaig.

"Glen Fiddich," he said. "I-C-K."

"H," said MacCaig. "He pronounces antisyzygy wrong, too."

"I'm interested in all the modern manifestations of literature, Beckett, Italo Svevo. I'm most interested at the moment in two European poets who are genuinely scientists and whose poetry is dependent upon science. Holub, a Czech, lives in New York and works as a clinical pathologist, and the Swede, Harry Martinson, who once wrote a reasonable poem, 'Aniara,' on the evacuation of earth after a nuclear explosion."

"His songs must be in thune with the world," said MacCaig.

"There has been a big shift in the images in poetry," said MacDiarmid. "I find scientific matters an endless source of comment, analogy, image. What I've tried to tell the young people here is that a young poet must be generally educated in the sciences, accept the technology. Any rejection, I think, won't lead to good poetry."

"They say you're as good as the Baird."

"The Baird," said MacCaig.

"Ah, well. That. There's no real comparison in the work, in the world in which we've been involved. But it can be said the Scotch independence has always been best expressed in poetry. I realized that the moment I began, leaping over Burns altogether and got back to Dunbar. Burns was a great songwriter, you know, but there was so much triviality in his work. A great popular poet. Scotland's most popular poet."

"What he means," said MacCaig, "is he's trying to be Scotland's most unpopular poet."

MacDiarmid then read me, by request, "A Vision of Myself," half lenses on his nose, stubby pipe in and out of his mouth, shiny knees crossed at the edge of his kilt. He stumbled on the word *animalcula*, as he would have to.

"You're a turrible mon," I said.

"Let's talk of other men," he said. "More coffee and . . . ?"

"The weather, Christopher," said MacCaig. "Do you like the weather here at all?"

11 · The Word That Makes Flesh

In Westminster, Maryland, Irving West, while being arrested for disorderly conduct after being engaged in a fist fight, blasphemed a cop.

Maryland's law against blasphemy dated to 1723. It was based on the 1656 English law which imposed a penalty for a first offense at having a hole bored in the tongue; second offense at having a B branded on the forehead; third offense at being executed, without benefit of clergy.

Instead of all that, Maryland's Judge Charles Simpson, after convicting Irving West of blasphemy in 1968, sentenced him to a fine of twenty-five dollars and thirty days in jail.

Having thirty days in jail to think about this law, Irving West (who was a fighter, remember) decided to appeal.

Maryland's law against blasphemy was declared unconstitutional by Carroll County Judge Edward Weant, Jr., early in 1969.

One may now blaspheme in Maryland.

Even at a cop.

A pacifist, being interviewed by his draft board, was asked the usual question: "What would you do if forty of your friends were about to be killed and only you could prevent it by grabbing a machine gun and using it against the enemy?"

The pacifist answered, "I'd wave the whole situation away with a magic wand."

Somewhat taken aback, the interviewer asked, "Where would you get a magic wand?"

And the pacifist answered, "The same place you'd get forty friends."

"Don't you sing that song," the captain of police said.

"It's not a song. It's a cheer."

"I don't care what it is. One dirty word out of you and we'll yank you off that stage so fuckin' fast you won't know what the fuck hit you, shithead."

We had already noticed the patrol wagon backed up to the stage door.

"All right," singer, cheerleader Country Joe McDonald said. "Leave me alone."

So he went on stage and did his gig in front of an audience of sixteen thousand people while the officer with the silver hair and the gold braid stood staring at him from the floor in front of the stage, arms akimbo, twenty uniformed policemen extending from each elbow, forty-one policemen in all, watching the performer on the lit stage rather than the sixteen thousand kids tiered in the dark.

And when it came time for Country Joe McDonald to lead his dirty-word cheer, with all these cops in front of him, the patrol wagon behind him in the alley, its door open, he did the obvious and shouted:

"Give me an L!"

"L!" roared back from the dark.

"Give me an O!"

"O!"

"Give me a V!"

"V!"

"Give me an E!"

"E!"

"And what have you got?"

And while Country Joe McDonald said absolutely nothing, just stood there on the stage, hands placidly folded over the guitar hanging from his shoulders, looking down at the silver-haired cop with the gold braid, arms akimbo, twenty cops extending from each elbow, sixteen thousand kids tiered in the dark shouted:

"Fuck! Fuuuuuuuck!!! Fuck!"

12   Joan Baez

The spirit of Man
is a bird in a cage,
That beats on the bars
Wi' a goodly rage.
—*Hugh MacDiarmid*

✦ ✦ ✦

She was young and she really was pretty, you know, and she was
uptight nearly all the time in those days, what with appearing before
mammoth crowds and sitting in jail cells and all.

Until that moment backstage I thought we would, *I* would never
see Joan Baez (born, Staten Island, New York, January 9, 1941). "Miss
Baze," as she called herself, as that restless kid-spirit, that blow-the-lid-
off-the-world (not with careful, distortable phrases), make-it-happy
feeling, she must have had bubbling inside her all the time, to be what
she was, to do what she had done.

Then*, pajong!*

Three of us were sitting cross-legged in the wings (Ira Sandperl, a
kindly professorial type in tweed who ran her Institute for the Study
of Nonviolence at Carmel, California; an Italian television producer
named Columbo, who had done a documentary on her, and your
observer). After the intermission she had decently, fairly brought the
audience back to listening again—"She is so pleasing," an over-forty
lady in the lobby had said during intermission to her date, "always
dressed so conservatively"—attention, by doing one song, as she did

everything decently and fairly, before introducing her old pals, the Charles River Valley Boys.

Ten years before, she had been a sixteen-year-old stick with a guitar traipsing after these big guys, singing with them when they would let her. Now an international star, she had called the wife of one of them the day before when she had got to town and suggested the boys drop by her sold-out concert, with their guitars.

She stood in the open end of the wing, out of sight of the audience, listening, really listening to them, one arm across her body, the other elbow resting on it, forearm raised to her face, the thumbnail of her right hand inserted tentatively between her teeth, the right heel of her beautiful beige shoe tapping the dirty stage floor with their rhythm. Near the beginning of that song, so the audience could hear it, she yahooed carelessly with that expansive voice, high, deep in her throat. Within seconds a hiss-whisper came through the curtain at her from one of her entourage, "Save your voice!" Toward the end of the song, she yahooed again, this time more carefully, softly without the vibrato or gargle or whatever that might charge her throat. And she applauded, clapping her hands flat against each other, straight in front of her face, so the boys, her old pals, would not only hear her but see her, when they looked.

During their second song, a wild and crazy thing, she tapped her right heel again, somehow sedately but sharply, remarkably doing this little thing with the rhythm that appeared at first to be all of her, all she needed, dared to do, complete, while Ira turned his crinkly, weather-beaten face to us in the shadows, grinned, shrugged his shoulders, "This is what she's like. This is what she needs to do." In her straight, simple, exquisitely tailored, materialed, silk-lined beige dress her hips began moving, then stopped, everything stopped, hips and heel, and then she turned her back to the stage and kicked off her shoes (What are they on for? I never wanted them on) and began this crazy dance in this dark, open-ended curtain-box, the music, the stage lights behind her, a real heel-and-toe mud-stomp, (attended grammar school in Redlands, California) confined to a small area by the width of her skirt, the straightness of herself, the smallness of the area itself. Her shoulders were bobbing up and down, her hair bouncing on them against the backlight, her breathing was short, not thought about, not regular, surprised herself, apparently, at what she was doing.

What is she doing? How can she do this thing to herself halfway through a major performance, to her breathing, her hair, without having to make some excuse to the audience, let them know what she had been doing?

Uptight, sedately uptight the day before at the press conference, entering the room in a neat, dark blue suit, yellow blouse, sweet smile, she looked genuinely surprised and very pleased when the reporters stood for her. She sat on the divan in "that position" (Mrs. Youngwife pouring tea; uptight, holding herself back), the television lights bringing out the beautiful sheen of her below-the-shoulder, true-black hair, the luxuriance of her Mexican/British tanned skin.

In a half-circle in front of her sat the nice kids of the student press, wonderful-looking girls and boys who blushed a little when they asked her respectful questions. Behind them, the professional press, which had not arrived so early nor would stay so long. To one side, there was a tiresome old man obviously determined to show the kids up front how an old pro worked, who would rise with his question, remove his glasses and pace the floor, trying to ensnare her with his involute rhetoric like a slightly dyspeptic prosecutor.

"What kind of a singer are you?"

Uptight. "You tell me. What kind of a singer am I?"

"Miss Baez, you say you have withheld seventy-five percent of your taxes as a protest against the war in Vietnam. On what income?"

"You mean, how much do I make a year?"

"How much do you make?"

Uptight, uptight. "I don't know. Plenty. Perhaps you could ask my manager."

It was he who asked, "Are you an American patriot?" causing her to say something she regretted that night and the next day and which she talked worriedly about for some time after, "No, I am an American, but not a patriot," meaning, we finally figured out, "but I am not a Nationalist," going on to say she does not like that tribal thing which causes wars, which is not patriotism but which is nationalism. "I don't understand hippies" was reported as "I don't like hippies," which was also to bother her.

"What do you want with your success, your talent?"

The funny thing is that she looked at this prosecuting reporter type as if to say, under hooded eyes, "I knew you would be here, whoever you are. . . ."

"I want people to stop murdering each other."

Only one question, from all the press, touched upon music.

She answered, "For me, there gets to be less and less of a separation between my song and my politics. Life is made worth living by integrating everything you like."

She announced that December 18 (1967), she would take part in one more peace demonstration.

She said to the student press, "We thought it would be fun to spend Christmas in jail."

She said, "It isn't just the American role in Vietnam, or because of Vietnam that I can't consider myself totally loyal. If I were dropped in Hanoi I'd say the same thing: You've been trying this violence for twenty years now, and it hasn't gotten you anywhere. I'm not against the government. I'm against violence."

She said, "Do I ever sing a song just because I want to sing a song? Yes, I do. Sometimes, by myself, for four or five hours. I found in jail I could pour it out by hiding in the shower and singing there. It's the only place I had ever sung the blues—in a jail shower stall."

Watching, listening, you did get some sense of this girl, this slip of a girl with a cradle voice like few mothers ever have and a metallic backbone like few fathers ever have.

Alone together the day after her concert we discussed the irony of her being in opposition to many essential ideas of society, such as violence, but not, like many of her followers, in opposition to her immediate family.

"That's right, you know. My mother and sister were in jail with me this last time, as demonstrators, too."

Her Scottish-English maternal grandfather was an Episcopal minister; her Mexican paternal grandfather a Methodist minister.

"Dad wanted to be a minister, too, but he got interested in math."

Her father, in fact a Ph.D. in physics, devoted much of his life to UNESCO.

"My father was a bit too straight-laced. He'd have a purple fit if there were wine on the table. Thought we were all going to be drunks. I guess now one of my sisters smokes. That's as far as vice goes in our family." (Attended high school in Palo Alto, California.)

"But they really love us, the parents. We were never given reason to doubt that. And despite all we went through as teenagers, we really love them back."

She said, "The key to everything is that real love will get rid of our fears. Fear is what destroys everything. It causes violence. Love is to be able to give without asking for anything back."

"How do you sustain love?"

"You just keep trying," she answered. "I admit that I have violent fantasies, violent dreams, but I just keep trying. It's a good life."

Apparently she felt that if the government were truly representative of the people, it would never commit violence, which is truly questionable.

"But I'm not against democracy, the way it sounded the other day at the press conference. I just don't think we've ever made democracy work."

So before the concert Sunday night before two thousand people, Joan Baez sat in a huge queen's chair in her dressing room, uptight, quietly, sedately again, her eyes going from round to half-shuttered, skin over cheekbones white beneath her tan, fingers clutching the chair arms like a kid in a dentist chair, wishing the next period of time away.

"If there were no violence, I would not sing," she admitted. "I would run a school for little kids."

When it was time she walked very slowly to the stage, took the guitar from Ira without stopping or changing her pace, sleepwalked out into the lights of the stage, into the applause, into the big "Hi" of the audience.

Then that crazy little, shy, diffident half-salute of hers. "I have been a nonviolent soldier since I was fourteen," she had said.

She stood before the microphone in an exhausting, punishing, energy-sapping, knees-bent, slightly hunched position, right ear forward, listening to herself, listening to the house, sensitive to the tone of her guitar through its own mike, to whatever came up from the house, love and respect, hate and suspicion, telling her audience, finally, after a few songs of listening to them, "There's something very old-homey about this place, isn't there?"

During the intermission she ran through, rehearsed the one and only time, the song she was to do with the Charles River Valley Boys.

Then in the second half, the crazy dance she began and kept up in the wings, the flurry-rustle of her dress against her nylons, the rapid sound of her breath, the noise of her shoeless feet beating on the floor like a bat frantic in an attic, trying to find a window, get out to the light.

Lord, she turned, danced, pranced, stomped out into the shadows of the back of the stage, confined no longer, mud-stomped there until the audience saw her, began to applaud, then stomped forward, coming up into the light behind her old pals with their guitars, surprising them, who had not known why the audience was applauding suddenly in the middle of their song, perhaps had been hearing this frantic beating behind them, she now doing this happy kid-dance jump around them, through them, not touching them, never letting them know just where she was, a girl being a kid, a kid being a dancing Indian, anyone being happy, exuberantly apolitically happy, letting herself go, heel-and-toeing it for all those crazy bars, stretching her figure suddenly into a pretty pose, a tableau in the light at the last chord, holding the pose only as long as the chord lasted. Coming offstage, the Charles River Valley Boys were grinning, shaking their heads, laughing, looking back at her, old pals surprised.

Shoeless, she readjusted her mike, sang "Yesterday," thoroughly loose now, talked about her most recent experience, "a couple of weeks ago, when I was in jail," with warmth and love and humor. She sang "The Sisters of Mercy," by Canadian poet, novelist, singer Leonard Cohen, and "Gossamer," by herself, words by Nina Dusehek, a San Francisco housewife. She put her guitar down and ended the concert with "Freedom Now!" ("Na na na naa!" was she teaching it to them?), while the audience clapped hands and joined in as they went along, got the hang of it.

Her encore, still shoeless, her guitar hanging from her shoulders again, was "We Shall Overcome." The audience knew that one. They joined in without invitation.

✦ ✦ ✦

"I'm thoroughly ashamed of myself," Joan Baez said. "I shouldn't have hit him."

It was a year and a half later, July 1970.

She sat on the divan in the living room of her parents' house, now Mrs. Youngwife in fact. Her beautiful hair had been chopped off with pregnancy as the excuse. On the coffee table in front of her was a glass of wine, which she did not touch. On her knee was her beautiful son, Gabriel.

Almost immediately after the wedding, her husband, David Harris, had begun serving a three-year sentence in a federal penitentiary for draft resistance.

And, alone with her baby one night in her house in California, a man she described as "suffering from liquor and drugs" broke in and threatened her and Gabriel.

"Screaming like any other red-blooded American girl would have done," she reported, she surprised the intruder by attacking him with her fists and feet, hitting him and kicking him with all the force and might at her command.

He ran from the house.

"I suppose I could have gotten rid of him just by screaming," she now said. "I suppose."

Her face was a little harder then, at twenty-nine, and a little sadder, and when it was in repose it literally fell and I caught myself looking for the touch of bitterness in the corners of the mouth, and maybe I saw it beause I was looking for it. I couldn't conceive of her kicking off her shoes and raising the dust behind a theater curtain, in a wild, unrestrainable dance.

"Today is sort of a celebration. David is one-third through his prison sentence. He's been in jail a year today. And see? We're all alive and well."

Since Harris had gone to prison, besides Gabriel she had produced a long-playing record, *David's Album*, "full of the songs David likes best," and it had been sentimentally effective. "Glad Bluebird of Happiness" was followed by "Green, Green Grass of Home" followed by "Will the Circle Be Unbroken?"

A not very good book, *Goliath*, had been published under his name.

"I'd like to say that nonviolence has made a great thrust and things are much better now, but it just isn't true. Chaos is what is."

At that time, there were five hundred and fifty men in federal prisons for draft resistance. And it was termed "resistance" not "evasion." An estimated thirty thousand men had evaded the draft by fleeing to Canada. Unknown numbers had fled to Sweden, Mexico, Africa.

"In the high school in Palo Alto now I'm considered a middle class, bourgeois, racist pig. They say 'Let's do something real. Let's make firebombs.'" She handed Gabriel over to her mother. "More violence.

"The Mafia started as a group protecting the peasants," Joan Baez said. "And they had to get guns, turn to violence. And now you have the Mafia. Force has to become evil, no matter how nobly it begins.

"People have said I should leave the country. What good could I do if I left it?

"The country is not important to me at all. But the people of the country are."

And she said, "The lie of this country is that they preach to you in the schools the virtue of rugged individualism while molding you and molding you and molding you.

"The only rugged individualists in this country are in jails these days."

✦ ✦ ✦

Not long after David Harris completed his three-year jail sentence, with time off for good behavior, he and Joan Baez separated.

13   Solstice

Charles, just before being made Prince of Wales in July, 1969, was interviewed by a wire-service reporter at Wales' Aberystwyth College.
"There have been several previous monarchs whose qualities I would like to have," said the Prince. "But it is very difficult, because I haven't."
Charles was the first member of the English royal family to attend university.

✦ ✦ ✦

I arrived in Quebec City late at night on what Hemingway might have called a brave airplane. It was just before Christmas, snowing furiously, with a high wind. We sashayed into landing with all the exaggerated movements in the airplane's waist you would expect from Mae West entering a room where Raquel Welch was already present. Crossing to the terminal in wind and snow was so cold one had to disassociate oneself emotionally from one's skin.

If you asked the temperature, people looked at you as if you were questioning their federal constitution when in fact you were only questioning your own. They did not tell you the temperature, as a kindness. The temperature was so important, like death itself, one did not explicitly speak of it.

The next day the newspaper story on page thirty-six was to say something like, "Mini-blizzard a nuisance." On one side of town someone banged up his car, it was reported; on the other side, one inferred, an old man looking through his window decided right then to die of old age.

Nevertheless what I saw through the taxi window on the way to the wonderful Hotel Frontenac, the city in the swirling snow, was too beautiful to be missed, too great a contrast from Florida where I had just been, so, once at the hotel, I bundled up and took myself on a forced march around the Old City.

Anyone who builds a Santa town that doesn't look like Old Quebec is no builder of Santa towns: grey stone houses, buildings, snuggled against each other on narrow, winding streets on a mountainside, lights falling from their windows onto the snow outside, smoke from their chimneys testifying to the spirit of Man within, while outside snow beat furiously against lit street lights. One would almost look for Prancer and Dancer, or Marley's ghost, or a toy soldier.

There were only three other people out in the weather in Quebec City that night.

A young man, I suspect a citizen of the United States obeying Socrates, having left his nation when he could not agree with it, possibly a draft resister, a seeker after peace and perhaps truth and wisdom with a stuffed knap-sack on his back walking into the city passed me going uphill. He was rugged enough for anything. His face was wind-burned and he had a bulky sweater under his canvas windbreaker, and good boots. I did not worry about him. If he did not find peace or truth or wisdom that night he looked strong enough to take another day of lies and foolishness with the rest of us.

A girl stood in the wind on the side of the square. Magnificent dark eyes were visible over the turned-up collar of her ankle-length fur coat.

"Pardon me, sir," she asked in schoolbook French. "Do you know where The Homestead is?"

"Ah, you tourists," I answered in English. "You never give up."

Through the swirling snow, the nuisance mini-blizzard, her eyes changed to eternally memorable mirth. We laughed loudly together in the wind.

"You're a tourist, too!" she exclaimed in pure Kensington English. "Who else would be out on such a night?"

I didn't worry about her, either. One ought never worry about tourists.

Turning a corner near the top of the mountain I was caught by a blast of wind.

While regaining my footing I became aware of a soldier, in battle dress, standing in the middle of the sidewalk. We were mutually startled. A machine gun strapped over his shoulder was in the crook of his arm.

The sign on the building he was guarding read: United States of America Consulate.

His eyes, snow-caked lids and lashes, were utterly miserable. I worried about him. There was no sentry box for him, not even a doorway recessed out of the wind.

I said to the sentry: "Merry Christmas."

It took him three tries to speak.

His fourth try was a hoarse whisper releasing a full, body-length shiver.

"Sir. Merry Christmas. Sir."

✦ ✦ ✦

MERRY CHRISTMAS, MISTER POKAT

Have a nice weekend, Al.
Merry Christmas, Mister Pokat.
(hear them sing)
Merry Christmas, Al.
women's boney hands have
snaked over the counters of junk,
for weeks,
one elbow out as a flank to

ward off Scarsdale
(hear them ring)
there's always counterhelp

so cold you'd
think it was a national emergency
pour this guy/that into a taxi.
send her home.
(you were right again, Mister Huxley):
it's Christmas eve
and all the world is drunk.

don't forget, though,
our dear Miss Purdy
always had trimmed her tree
by december eighth

Santa, you know, has a cockeyed,
beery look, red nose and roseola.
all this foolishness about Prancer and Dancer
is like putting a six-pack salesman
behind the wheel of a 220SL
to make children laugh
precisely
how many friends
have you got?
seven airmail and
twenty-two regular
please

in a ballroom
in a hotel
downtown, uptown

office girls
in gold lamé
waltz
frug and
bugaloo with each other
having sprouted wings,
front and back,
'tween five and eight
anyway, he whips over the roofs when
other bounders with red noses
would be prudently visiting their married daughter
(sleigh bells ring)
all I want is my usual seat
my scotch and water
my financial page
skis from Groton,
skis from Yale;
girls on their way to
nice-looking kids:
using Christmas to live,
not to strangle
in a scarf
(making spirits rise)
using Christmas to go
someplace
where people aren't.
young eyes dark
with the secret knowledge of
where people aren't.

inflation, Mister Pokat.
credit spending, Mister Pokat.
federal reserve, Mister Pokat.

merry christmas, Mister Pokat.
did you tip the doorman
did you tip the
did you tip

the living room is a clutter
the den is a clutter
even the bedroom is a clutter
(you'd better not pout)
christmas is universal:
it makes a mess everywhere.

the cities smell of smoke now
some of the boys are gone now
(you'd better not cry)
and that noise you hear
is the new left
demonstrating on the roof

children, children, if you don't
be quiet I'll
the glow of children's faces
as their monetary eyes
calculate five and tens:
five is for being a good boy;
ten is for being quiet.
a four-year-old boy, though
—and this is the beautiful thing—
dressed so warmly he toddles like
a little stuffed bear
through the wonderland of Christmas lights
in the city park
looking

looking
like us all
asks so patiently,
and where is the little Boy?

all I want is my usual seat
my scotch and water
some work to do
tra la la la la
la la la la
in exactly one week,
Mister Pokat will say tonight,
we'll be singing *Auld Lang Syne*
in memory
of those we forgot
la la la la la
la la la la
to send Christmas cards

14   Donovan

Tom Winslow in Kansas received a bill from a department store for $00.00. Not realizing fast enough his account number had slipped into the maw of a computer, he ignored the bill.

The following month he got another bill for $00.00. Which he also ignored.

The third month, the bill for $00.00 was marked Past Due. He circled the $00.00 in red and sent it back.

The fourth month a stiff note accompanied the bill saying he was liable for civil suit and if he did not pay $00.00 immediately, the department store would hand his account over to attorneys.

So, he sent the department store a check for $00.00.

And heard no more about it.

Which was the first proof we had that anyone can communicate with a computer, if you just take your time, and think about it.

✦ ✦ ✦

In 1964, at the Newport Folk Festival, a young man strolling down a hotel corridor towards the elevator found the door to Donovan Leitch's room open.

Inside, Donovan was on the bed with his guitar. "Hey," the young man said.

Donovan said, "Hi."

"You going to sing a song?"

Donovan pulled the guitar onto his lap, and sang.

> When you're feelin' kind of lonesome in your mind
> With a heartache followin' you so close behind

Call out to me as I ramble by
I'll sing a song for you
That's what I'm here to do
To sing for you.

Donovan Leitch was born in Glasgow, Scotland, on February 10, 1946. He contracted polio when he was three years old. At ten, he was moved to Hatfield, England.

Very soon thereafter he "cut an outadere" and hit the road with his friend, Gypsy Dave, singing and laboring around England. By the time he got to Manchester he was dirty-enough looking to be picked up on suspicion of stealing cigarettes and candy from a movie theater. He spent two weeks in Strangeways Prison, which was not a nice place, washing and eating his way into an acquittal. He said he wrote two songs during those two weeks.

Soon he was back in Hatfield, singing around the clubs, "gettin' slowly unknown," in his words. Then he met a good guy named Peter Eden who brought him to another good guy, Geoff Stephen, a songwriter at Southern Music, who brought him to still another good guy, Terry Kennedy. These three were his original managers and producers.

In 1964 at the Newport Folk Festival not many knew much about Donovan Leitch, or even what he looked like.

When the night has left you feelin' cold and sad
I will show you that it cannot be so bad
Forget the one who went and made you cry
I'll sing a song for you
That's what I'm here to do
To sing for you . . .

sang the kid with the bum leg on the bed.

✦ ✦ ✦

"No one sees Donovan."

Three years later I had the distinct impression I had been invited and had agreed to interview Donovan backstage during a major concert.

I hadn't realized he had been turned into Snow White and the Seven Managers.

By then, my son, *der Gingel*, three years old, aped Donovan pretty well, and pretty continuously:

I'll take you ridin' in my cah-cah

(A little white plastic thing he scooted along rugs. One wheel had fallen off).

The horn goes beep-beep

(*Der Gingel* had put the wheel from the car into his piggy bank, which was a dog).

Engine goes brrp-brrp

(Oh, boy, did it ever, night and day).

Back seat, front seat

(So *der Gingel* would try to straddle the back of the front seat, while riding in my cah).

When you're ridin' in my cah.

There was this girl I knew whose eyes would go absolutely plastic at hearing Donovan singing:

> I'm just mad about Saffron
> Saffron's mad about me
> They call me Mellow Yellow
> That's right . . .

And this man about forty-five, my editor, Ian Forman, looked very serious when he asked, "Do you know Donovan's 'Sunny South Kensington'? It's pretty funny, you know."

It had also been arranged that a photographer, Steve Hansen, would be accompanying me backstage.

The Seven Managers put on a pretty good show for us. The sight of cameras apparently sent them wild.

"Out, out," said the Manager in Charge of Breakfast.

"Don't you shoot that thing," said the Manager in Charge of Whatever Happens after Breakfast.

"No cameras backstage," said the Manager in Charge of Lunch.

"Cap it up. Put it away," said the Manager in Charge of Naptime.

"You're not a real photographer," said the Manager in Charge of Late Afternoon. "You're not old enough."

"Put it away. Right now," said the Manager in Charge of Supper.

Steve said, "If I were any older, I would have left already."

The Manager of All the Managers, Ashley Kozak, said, someone finally addressing me, "We grant no interviews. My office should have told your office. We've turned down *Life* and *Look* and all sorts of people. Donovan hasn't spoken to anyone since he entered the country. And he won't."

Besides the seven managers, there were between twenty and thirty uniformed police and firemen in the building, plus thirty ushers and usherettes. From what I could see, they were all being directed by the Seven Managers to withstand the onslaught of a single photographer.

Last I saw of Steve, he was being pursued by four people with flashlights.

He got some great shots from the rafters.

✦ ✦ ✦

Janis Ian, sixteen years old and not many more than that inches high, billed as a guest star, carried the whole first half of the concert.

She dedicated one song to guidance counselors.

Then there was Donovan for the second half.

Dressed in a white, ankle-length robe, some sort of burnoose, I guess (a time-to-retire nightgown), sandals, he stood at a microphone on a bed of giant-blossomed flowers, red, white, and yellow. His musicians were behind him on the softly red-lit stage. A saffron hand-kerchief, or scarf or something, was tied to, hanging from his left wrist. When he wasn't playing his guitar he would run the scarf through his fingers, pull it, twist it, flap it.

Mostly respected as a composer, his melodies and lyrics, sung by nearly everybody, were at the top of the charts. His own voice, soft and gentle, could have an amazing timbre, virility.

And he could actually play the guitar. His "Tangerine Puppet" was strictly an instrumental, which he performed if not with Segovian subtlety at least with Donovan earnestness.

His audience was able to identify each song during the evening within the first three chords, and usually applauded the choice as well as the performance.

The kid with the bum leg sitting on the bed in Newport singing to his guitar, "When you're feeling sort of lonesome in your mind," had been packaged by a berserk computer run by Seven Managers in Charge of the Person as Property.

✦ ✦ ✦

The door to Donovan's dressing room was open.

There were not too many kids standing outside his door.

"Hey," I said.

Donovan said, "Hi." From inside the room he held a cigarette out to me. "Want a cigarette? An English one?"

After he lit the Rothman for me he said, "I need a rose."

Ashley Kozak, The Manager in Charge of All Managers, handed him a beautiful red rose, just off bud.

Donovan broke the stem of the rose with his fingers. He tried to put the stem of the rose through the buttonhole in my lapel, which was stitched.

"It's a phony," Ashley said. "It's a phony buttonhole."

"Shh, Ashley," said Donovan. "You get too excited."

He tucked the rose behind my lapel. The rose fell.

I caught the rose and put the stem through a buttonhole in my vest.

"Maharishi Mahesh Yogi," I said.

"That's the whole thing," Donovan answered. "That's everything."

"When did you go to him?"

"I didn't go to him. He came to me. He came to all of us."

"You mean, the Rolling Stones, the Beatles?"

"Yes. All of us. He came to us, one by one, because he feels we're the leaders of youth. Sort of."

"When was this?"

We were leaning against the door jambs, facing each other within the doorway.

"Two or three weeks ago. In LA. We spent four very revealing days with him."

"He's a very great man," said Ashley. "They're building a thing to him, you know. In London."

"But he's gone back to India now," Donovan said. "We're going to go there as soon as we can get away."

"Your garb predates Maharishi Mahesh."

"My garb?"

"Your robes."

"Oh, yes. Everything really was before him. It was a mutual thing, really. See, I was already on that route anyway. I was looking for Maharishi. I was already on that route before I met him. I mean, meditation, things like that."

A Manager in Charge of After Concerts handed Donovan an orangeade.

"Go interview him. Please. For me. Go talk with him. You see. Maharishi can control an interview. He has the language, the thought, to control a situation. This is why I don't like interviews. I don't feel

I'm ready yet, I have the language, to control them, to say what I want without someone misquoting, distorting what I mean. I don't feel I can establish the rapport with anyone, to really talk. I feel I have established rapport with you, personally."

"What do you want to say?"

"Don't take drugs. Tell everybody not to take drugs. They must not take drugs."

"Even marijuana?"

"Even marijuana. There's no need to. See, India has the experience with it. Eleven hundred years ago they understood atomic power: just Man. Here kids don't know what they're doing. It's a route. Some take this, that. They don't know what they're doing."

Through the doorway a kid said, "There are teachers here who supposedly teach you how to use them, the differences."

"Yeah, but there's still no need. Learn to relax, to meditate, to do other things. Physical things. There's no need to drop out. All the old idiots, the ones who make the wars, are going to die off. They're doing so. All we have to do is wait."

A girl named Donna came to the door and gave Donovan a huge glass ring.

He put it on his finger.

"It picks up colors." He held the ring on his finger next to my chest. "You can see his blue coat through it."

Then he held it to the edge of his cup, perhaps to try to see the orange drink as Mister Dee-Lish must have seen it.

"All this surprises you, doesn't it?" he said. "What I say about the drugs. I'm serious. That's no way to God. People want to go to the moon. That's no way to God either. Maybe sitting in the chair on the way there, they'll see God, if they meditate enough, or in preparing for this wonderful thing."

"Does this come from the Maharishi?"

"No. It comes from me. I'm serious. I was on this route before him. I mean that."

"Do you want me to say you were, in your words, on the other route, that you experimented with drugs?"

"You bet. Of course say it. How else would I know? It's the wrong route. You don't see God. You can fool yourself, and one thing does lead to another. The route is to relax, rest, exercise, meditate. You feel great."

"Who's Gypsy Dave?"

"A very close friend of mine, sort of a blood brother. We hit the road together, you know."

"What's his name?"

"Just Dave."

"Is he still around?"

The Hickory album, *Catch the Wind*, listed Gypsy Dave as a kazoo player. The more recent Epic albums, do not list him.

"Sure. Not here tonight, because of a thing. But he's still around."

"Was he with you during the two weeks you spent in Strangeways Prison?"

"No," Donovan said, "He was more clever than I."

> When you feel you can't make it anymore
> With your head bowed down you're starin' at the floor
> Search out to me with your weary eyes
> I'll sing a song for you
> That's what I'm here to do
> To sing for you.

"Hey." Donovan put his hands in my jacket pockets. "What have you got in your pockets?"

In one pocket was a Vicks inhaler. I'd had a headcold. Looking at the inhaler in his hand, Donovan looked shocked.

"No drugs," he said. "Remember: no drugs."

✦ ✦ ✦

Steve Hansen was waiting for me in the theater lobby.

"What happened to six out of the seven managers?" I asked.

"They're next door in a bar," Steve said. "Having a drink with Donovan's dad."

15   Rules

In April 1966, the Cambridge (Massachusetts) Licensing Board issued a fourteen page booklet setting certain rules for taxi drivers. A taxi driver may not consume food or drink while waiting at a stand. He may not smoke while transporting passengers. If he wears a cap, it must be a regulation chauffeur's cap. His badge must be worn on the left side of his chest. He must be able to speak and write English intelligibly. He many not wear a beard or an extreme haircut.

That was the summer it was absolutely impossible to get a taxi in Cambridge, Massachusetts. There weren't any on the streets. There weren't any drivers.

By fall, the rule book had been thrown away, and there were taxis again.

◆ ◆ ◆

In the reading room of Widener Library, Harvard University, a girl sat most of the afternoon waiting for a boy beside her to get to a point on his economics paper where he felt he could leave it. She wore an open black sweater on top of a red sweater and he was in his shirt sleeves, tweed coat over the back of his chair. Their hair was long. Hers was tied behind her neck to show red gypsy earrings. At first she read the *New York Times*. Then she sighed and waited and told him by a look she was bored, but he didn't mind. When a boy in lederhosen walked by, going into the reference room, her eyes grew wide and she picked up her book, *History of Africa*. Her wedding ring was minute and there was no engagement ring.

✦ ✦ ✦

William Alfred was an ordinary citizen of Harvard University. There was some esthetic in Cambridge which still respected chastity and championed celibacy.

When you visited William Alfred at his Cambridge bachelor house on Athens Street, in the shade of Leverett House Tower, he sat you in an uncomfortable, wheezing chair in his back living room, then soothed your discomfort with a large Irish whiskey.

Between his chair and your own is a table. He proceeds to dart about the house collecting the books to which he refers as if to show you he does not lie, their existence is real. He piles them on the table between you, a solid wall of must-read. In fact, as he discourses in his chair he sinks from view behind this ever heightening wall of books.

It is at least two hours before he tells you you are sitting in the chair Robert Frost always preferred when he came to visit. It is indicated to you that it was Frost's literary weight that broke the spring in the chair upon which you sit. Inappropriate Frostian lines regarding Spring and springs choke in your throat. "And make us happy in the darting bird. . . . The meteor that thrusts in with needle bill. . . ." The strong are saying nothing. In the seat of learning, you must respect both history and sentiment.

There was something about William Alfred, perhaps the big, happy eyes in a balding head, which gave him the look of an altar boy with a frog in his pocket.

A teacher at Harvard College, English 10, Beowulf to Present, William Alfred was also the author of the critically and commercially successful play, *Hogan's Goat.*

"I'm not a writer who teaches, but rather a teacher who writes," he said. "Now I could leave teaching if I want, but I won't. I like it too much."

Born into a Brooklyn Irish family, William Alfred was graduated from Saint Francis Preparatory School in 1940. In January 1943, after two years at Brooklyn College, he was drafted into the army. He was assigned to the tank corps and sent for desert training in Arizona. That was just after the North African campaign had been won.

He was assigned to the motor pool.

"I never learned to drive, you know. Once I threw out something called throw-out batteries I wasn't supposed to."

He was then assigned to language school, where he was taught Bulgarian.

Then he was assigned to the South Pacific.

He lessened the boredom of military life in the South Pacific by writing poems for *American Poet*. He also wrote long letters to Washington, in Bulgarian.

"It's the fright of my existence that some student will dig up those old poems of mine. They were dreadful."

He did not characterize his letters in Bulgarian.

With the G. I. Bill he graduated from Brooklyn College. He took his masters and Ph.D. ("Anglo-Saxon Poems on Religious Themes") from Harvard.

While *Hogan's Goat* was in rehearsal, William Alfred was scheduled for twenty hours of classroom teaching a week, all from Monday to Wednesday. Each Wednesday night he flew to New York, where he remained until Sunday.

"Very exhilarating. Did my reading on the airplanes and during rehearsals, listening with one big ear."

William Alfred was a lay priest of the Roman Catholic Church. His friends called him Mr. Alfred.

Harvard students went to New York in droves to see the play.

"They felt they shared in its success with me—the miracle of the play's working out."

While teaching, he had lunch with students in the Kirkland House dining hall every day. Students, seeing lights on in his house behind Leverett Towers, are apt to drop in on him, with their dates, at all hours.

From the university students alone, Mr. Alfred received twenty to forty play manuscripts a year, to read, judge, discuss, plus poems and novels.

It was also his pleasure to rescue clocks from here and there (he also owned a home in Dublin, Ireland) and fix them persistently. His house on Athens Street had so many ticking clocks the overall effect was that milliseconds were being tocked.

After he finishes describing the books he built in a wall between you and him, safely into his third Irish whiskey, Mr. Alfred savors the work of his students as he might a wine, by its years.

"Then, in the class of '63: I think you'll be hearing a lot about a man named D__ B__ very soon. He's done a play about Harvard undergraduate life, suicide, the various versions of it." There was nothing visible of Mr. Alfred then but the top of his bald head behind the wall of books he had built between you and him. "And D__C__. He's done three plays. Philosophical, but as funny as you can have. E__C__ is one. And T__ B__, who was here as a graduate student, is a fine playwright."

Mr. Alfred has sunk totally from view. Mr. Alfred is silent. The unsynchronized clocks keep up their chatter.

Finally, from Mr. Alfred sunk in his chair behind his wall of books, after his having spoken lovingly and admiringly of his students, you hear him say, with the musing disgust of age increasing by each tick of his furious clocks: "Young people: they have the energy of drunks, and they don't even drink!"

◆ ◆ ◆

Folksinger Tom Rush and I went into the bar of the nightclub in which he was to sing that night, to have a beer.

Posters of Tom were stuck to the bar mirror.

As waitresses came on duty, we could hear them gushing glandularly about getting to hear, getting to see, maybe even getting to touch Tom Rush that night, their very own selves.

When a waitress finally came over we each ordered a beer.

She brought only one beer. She placed it in front of me.

We asked her to bring another, for Tom.

She never did.

Without having touched my beer, finally I waved to the waitress in the empty bar. I gestured she should bring another beer.

The waitresses were talking about Tom Rush.

We waited.

No other beer was brought.

I caught her eye and gestured again.

"That long-haired kid in the corner booth," one of the waitresses said, referring to Tom Rush.

"Well, I'm not gonna serve him," our waitress said, flouncing some menus on the bar. "You can if you want."

"Not me."

Tom grinned. "Never mind. I don't want a beer that much."

16 The Trouble with Harry

I was sitting on a workbench in the studio beneath his house.

Kahlil Gibran, the international gold medalist sculptor, godson and nephew of the mystical poet of the same name, was working on his Reclining Nude.

Dusting the nude's leg with a rag, apropos of nothing, in the silence of his basement studio, Gibran said: "Only Man has the brilliance to make a nuclear bomb. Only Man has the foolishness to use it. And only Man has the greatness to recover from having used it."

✦ ✦ ✦

In his later years, Harry Kemp was given the title, "Poet of The Dunes," at a town meeting by the people of Provincetown, Massachusetts. Harry wore the title as others might the rank of Ambassador. He enjoyed all the privileges and fulfilled all the responsibilities.

When Harry had first arrived in the town, a young man fresh from Greenwich Village, he was poetically exhilarated by the sweep of the sand dunes. This was in the early 1900s. In exuberance, he pulled off all his clothes and, delighting in his freedom, in his bare pelt, ran across the sand, up the side of one dune, over its top to tumble uncontrollably down the other side.

He sprawled in the middle of a church picnic.

His literary distinction derived chiefly from his having run away with the wife of a novelist. (When Harry, being a gentleman, saw fit to apprise the novelist of his plans, the novelist said, "Here. Take the coffee pot, too." The affair was short-lived, as the novelist is apt to be better heeled than the poet; the woman shortly realized Harry was never to have a coffee pot of his own).

His poems received a limited circulation in Greenwich Village in the 1920s. But no one ever thought Harry had much posterity.

None could calculate how Harry's restless spirit would outlast his natural life.

He banged together an incredible shack on the dunes. What Harry meant by feet was not what a carpenter means by feet; Harry's meter was less certain. He lived there by himself until his very last days when he was induced to occupy a shack in town for two months during the winters.

In all seasons, all weathers, he would rise with the sun and jump naked into the surf. He would read an hour of Greek and an hour of Latin before breakfast. The mornings were spent writing poetry, putting his gentle thoughts into hard forms. In the afternoons he would trek across the dunes to town, sit in a warm corner of a bar (everyone had a drink for Harry; he was usually blue with cold), blink red-rimmed eyes at the world and jot on bits of paper.

In the last years his poetry got no farther than the town paper, now defunct. His metaphors sometimes coupled Christ with someone in the town who had been kind to him.

Harry was more than loyal to town history. He advocated it.

Annually, when it was much too cold, Harry would coax a variety of people out to New Beach, now called Herring Cove Beach, I guess it being no longer new. There he would reenact the Pilgrims' landing. Men, boys and girls, in whatever Harry had been able to scrounge as costumes (knee stockings over blue jeans) would row out a way and then, on signal from Harry, come back through the surf to shore.

In a laurel wreath, and carrying a staff, Harry would greet them. He would step forward and shout into the wind his verses of greetings to the Pilgrims.

At this point in Harry's life, his verses were not concise.

"For heaven's sake, Harry. Hurry up," would be heard muttered from the Pilgrims, standing knee deep in the surf, shivering in all their parts.

"Oh, no! Not another verse, Harry!"

Harry never heard their imprecations.

"Harry! It's cold!"

At one time the town young invited him to a beach party. Harry sat against the dune, old eye pockets ridged down to his mouth, watching them, loving them, working on a poem about them which subsequently appeared in the town newspaper.

> The only promiscuous thing there
> Was the sand.
> There was nothing as promiscuous
> As the sand.

The story of his battle over *Mayflower II* was reported at great length in a national magazine.

The replica of the original *Mayflower*, mostly a British gesture of goodwill to her forgiven colony, was scheduled to sail the original route from England to America. However, the plan as announced was for *Mayflower II* to depart authenticity by bypassing Provincetown, where the original *Mayflower* stopped first, and go directly on to Plymouth up the coast.

Harry revolted.

Ancient though he was, he took up collections to support his protest. Daily (some say hourly) he besieged the Queen of England, Elizabeth II, with verses on behalf of historic authenticity, cabled to Buckingham Palace. He insisted in every form of poetry ever devised that as the original *Mayflower* had called first at Provincetown, so must *Mayflower II*.

His verses of supplication to Her Majesty were ignored.

So he took some of the money he had collected and hired an airplane. During the annual festivities at Plymouth Rock, Harry flew over the rock in his rented airplane and bombed it with small paper bags of Provincetown sand. Throwing all caution to the wind as well, he had the young pilot circle the Rock many times. To the astonishment of the dignitaries gathered below, Harry made many direct hits.

That demonstration got Harry and his cause some attention.

Mayflower II did call at Provincetown before going to Plymouth. Town salts stood in the wind and the rain on a bluff and jeered Captain Villier's efforts to get the unwieldy ship around Race Point. Finally, historic authenticity be damned, *Mayflower II* had to be towed into Provincetown Harbor.

Harry was perfectly happy.

During his last few years a young lady in the town took care of Harry. She made sure he came in off the dunes in extreme winter. She gave him at least one hot meal a day.

Much to everybody's surprise, shortly before Harry died he became a Roman Catholic. Nobody could be sure whether it was the theology or the Latin that got him.

Harry's death revealed both elements in the town, in the world at that time, as well as something of his own universality.

The Catholics treated Harry to a decent wake at Nickerson's Funeral Home. They planned a nice funeral. They intended to plant Harry in consecrated ground.

The town young had different plans. It was not how Harry died, it was how Harry lived, as a free spirit insisted they. They expressed vast disappointment at Harry's having kicked over the traces of the free life and joined the fold at the last moment. They insisted that all Harry's life Harry had intended to be cremated.

They got nowhere with their argument. Cremation is forbidden by the laws of the Roman Catholic Church.

Harry, clean shaven, hair combed, in a yellowing white shirt, depressed jacket and unlikely neck tie, was laid out in the local parlor.

A few of the town young, beatniks, hippies, had a long, black, ancient Cadillac hearse. They lived in it. For the one hundred dollar purchase price, they had habitation, transportation and, depending upon where they chose to park it, a marvelous vehicle for offending whichever segment of Provincetown society had most recently scoffed at them.

The first evening of Harry's wake, after Nickerson Funeral Home was closed, a policeman patrolling discovered the funeral home had been broken into. He summoned the establishment.

The town young had absconded with Harry.

The establishment, having the power and belief that Harry really didn't want to be carted around that way, telephoned the police up-Cape: "Someone has kidnapped Harry."

Since the digging of the Cape Cod Canal, the Cape is rather like an island. It is joined to the mainland by two big bridges, the Bourne, and the Sagamore.

The Bourne police examined the vehicles coming off the bridges.

Sure enough, there was Harry respectfully laid out in the back of the big, black ancient hearse.

Harry was turned back at the Bourne Bridge.

The town young said they only wanted to cremate Harry, which was what Harry had wanted.

The town establishment sympathized with their interest in the matter, noted how much Harry had meant to the town young, noted the respect they had shown Harry by at least transporting him in a hearse, and did not press charges.

Harry was reensconced in Nickerson Funeral Home, admittedly looking awkward, undeniably out of place among the flowers and Muzak in his yellowing collar and a weather-beaten boney face.

No one dreamed the town young would try it again.

The second night the town young were smarter. They stayed off the main road which slowed them down. When they found their old hearse had not beaten the police to the bridge, they hid Harry in the woods.

They tried outwaiting the roadblock.

But it was no good. The police remained suspicious of every car coming off the bridge. They took it as a matter of pride that they could stop a corpse crossing one of two bridges.

Harry began to mellow in the hearse in the woods.

Thwarted by the police and nature, the town young had no choice but to drive Harry slowly back to Provincetown.

But still the battle over Harry's not resting in peace raged. His remains were fought over with scarce propriety.

The town young insisted that Harry ought not be subjected to any traditional formalities beyond his last. He had wanted to be cremated.

The establishment insisted Harry had made his choices, knew the rules, when he had become a Roman Catholic.

At the last possible moment the issue could be debated, someone found a paper out in Harry's shack on the beach, written in Harry's beautiful old hand. "My final wish as a Roman Catholic is to be cremated."

The town young scattered Harry's ashes over the dunes, where, it would seem, at least a part of Harry remains to this day.

17 Youngbodies

The only promiscuous thing there
Was the sand.
There was nothing as promiscuous
As the sand.

—Harry Kemp

✦ ✦ ✦

Handsome, impeccably dressed Society band leader Peter Duchin sipped his black coffee. "Society music is two-beat music played fast, so older people can cut the beat in half and walk around to it," he said. "In fact, we play very little of it.

"I have no idea what Society itself is. Everybody has his own idea of what Society is. What they usually mean is somebody they admire, or somebody who has something they haven't. Society is an envied few.

"If you play ten debutant parties in a row across the country, you see the same kids there. Philadelphia, Detroit, Chicago, Baltimore . . .

"If you had to categorize what their parents do, they'd be in business, banking, brokerage.

"If you go to Texas, the fact that someone has been there four generations means nothing in Society. Same in California.

"There are certain entrenched areas, notably Boston, Grosse Pointe, where how long your family has been there and been successful is still important.

"But even that doesn't make any difference to the younger generation. Not as much as it did in the 1950s, when I was in college.

"The dividing line today is not money, but social consciousness. In Society today, some have bread, and some don't. The fifth generation thing is nice but, by itself, it means nothing.

"What I'd call Society today is the establishment, usually comprised of people who have proven they've done something constructive, despite their breeding.

"Society has always been the admired people. The people youth admires today are the people who do things. Who are constructive, aware, and conscious.

"Those who are not conscious today simply are not admired."

✦ ✦ ✦

In 1969, of all Americans who owned a record album, eighty percent of them owned at least one by Frank Sinatra.

✦ ✦ ✦

"You see those guys," said Tony Dolan at a table down at Morey's.

There were three shaggier Yalies at a table against the wall passing a huge silver goblet among themselves, taking sips from it. The convention is that whoever lets the goblet touch the table has to pay for its refill.

At that time, Tony, also a Yale undergraduate, was making a heroic effort to counter the liberal folksingers by plucking a guitar himself and singing songs of more conservative message. A little lamb bleating in the wilderness then, Tony Dolan became a White House speechwriter for President Ronald Reagan.

"They do a stupid, Yale-traditional thing like that with utter seriousness," Tony said, "but if you asked them to stand up and sing 'God Bless America' they'd die of embarrassment."

✦ ✦ ✦

Shortly after marrying Yoko Ono, John Lennon went to court and had his name changed to John Ono Lennon. Oh, yes: he died by an assassin's bullet as John Ono Lennon.

The Beatle's middle name had been Winston.

✦ ✦ ✦

Tom O'Horgan directed the theater pieces *Hair* and *Futz* and something only a few hundred of us ever saw, called *Massachusetts Trust*.

Those of us who saw *Massachusetts Trust* were surprised by it. We had not been told what to expect.

There were at least three memorable moments of theater in *Massachusetts Trust*.

One was when a young man and a young woman were undressed and turned to face each other on the stage bathed only in light. The physical pride with which they stood there was absolutely stunning.

The audience, not having been told to expect anything prurient, saw nothing prurient.

"Oh, my God," said a middle-aged woman seated behind me. "They are so beautiful. That is so beautiful."

I asked Tom O'Horgan over lunch if there was anything genuinely, physically different about that generation, those who were being called kids into their thirties.

"Their bodies are remarkably efficient," Tom O'Horgan answered. "They're not queer, exhibitionist or any of those other things confused adults say about them.

"They are not sexually distinct enough to be any of those things.

"They are simply relaxed, utterly at home with themselves and each other. We have left them no mysteries, and therefore no images to create. They are themselves, natural, neutral in appearance, without any sexual mannerisms, role playing, point of view.

"Their relaxation, comfort with each other is about the only thing they have. And it is the one thing adult society wishes to bang out of them.

"But I can guarantee you, they will not respond to any authoritative effort to make them be what they cannot be.

"It is not just that they are incapable of masculine–feminine roles. It has to do with authority and control, to which these kids have a different, a passive response.

"For instance, to achieve a unison of movement in these kids, I have to foist upon them some sort of democratic method. I have to say 'we.'

"They can only do those things they have arrived at physically, through exercises. They can't be talked into anything.

"If I arbitrarily try to tell them to do something together, they won't. And they're right. They can't.

"They know better what their bodies can do."

✦ ✦ ✦

A marquee read: Rip Torn in *Coming Apart.*

✦ ✦ ✦

Speaking at Brandeis University, stage and film director Mike Nichols said: "Soon everyone in the country will be a director–except for certain strong-willed families, whose sons will become doctors.

"I find it startling that anyone you meet on the street can tell you the technicalities of making film. It's strange, this fashionable thing that making movies has become.

"I very much regret that film is becoming a cultist thing."

Your observer was not present when Mike Nichols made these remarks.

I saw the film of his appearance, made by Brandeis undergraduates.

Directed by Mike Schaeffer.

✦ ✦ ✦

And there was the vision presented of the world ending with a whimper rather than a bang: Julian Beck and Judith Malina's Living Theater.

It was excruciatingly boring.

The nearly-naked troupe entered the darkened stage from both sides more slowly than an idiot's thought. They carried lit incense sticks.

As the lights came up they crept off the stage and up the aisles. In the wake of their incense, they permeated the audience.

Sitting cross-legged onstage, Julian Beck began his litany.

"Stop the wars."

Endlessly, endlessly, endlessly he repeated the line.

An increasing section of the audience repeated the line after him.

"Freedom now."

Endlessly repeated.

"Free the blacks."

The members of the troupe, creeping through the audience like wraiths, eye-balling you like El Greco portraits scarcely come to life, the thick, heavy smell of the incense: mesmerizing, yes, but carried on at a pace so far below normal heart rate, breath rate, thought rate that it was only with the greatest difficulty that at least one member of the audience could force the necessary passivity upon oneself.

"Feed old men."

After well more than an hour of this essentially unmoving theater, a few members of the audience (rebelling? giving in?) started a few chants of their own.

"Vote with your feet!"

Endlessly, endlessly, Julian Beck would repeat these chants from onstage.

After an eternity, plus a few eons, Beck fell silent.

The members of the troupe drifted back onstage.

They dropped their burned-out incense sticks on the stage floor before him in an apparently ritualistic offering.

Then they began to walk in a slow circle around him. They hummed a single, low note.

Tightening the circle, they put their arms around each other's necks and waists. They swayed against each other.

A few at first, then scores from the audience went up onto the stage. They extended their arms to each other.

Tight circles of people compressed other tight circles of people. The hum became an endless groan.

The stage filled with tightly packed, slightly swaying upright human bodies, embracing, deeply layered concentric circles facing their own center, groaning.

There was no resolution of this. Population had hit infinity. Just people so tightly packed they could not separate or fall down or sway too much, sway voluntarily, or not sway.

Heads down, heads up they embraced each other on the darkened stage, and moaned fulsome despair.

✦ ✦ ✦

It was the biggest crowd ever at the Newport Jazz Festival weekend.

Paid attendance exceeded eighty-five thousand people. And there were more than one hundred thousand people outside the fences, come to camp on the slopes of the natural bowl, the hills overlooking Festival Field, and to hear, from there, the music.

It was an emergency on behalf of music.

Newport ran out of food. Restaurants closed. Newport roads were curb-to-curb cars. None were able to move.

No one could move without someone else's permission. Away from the upright crowd of Festival Field itself, the paid attendees, you could not walk without tripping over bodies rolled in blankets, asleep.

The biggest acts that year were Roland Kirk and his uniquely shaped horn, the incredibly witty, maybe too smart Mothers of Invention, Gary Burton, Sly and the Family Stone, Led Zeppelin and the "Number One Soul Brother," James Brown.

Festival Field, as it worked out, had one trained policeman for every one thousand kids.

It could have been the end of the world for some.

The Fuzz knew getting over the fence and through the tent holes was a game for the kids. They had the smarts to make a game of repelling them. When heads would appear over a fence, the Fuzz would raise their nightsticks and start forward with mock ferociousness. The heads would shriek obscenities and drop.

A beautiful young woman appeared through a hole in the fence. She blinked around, with great dignity and aplomb, at having finally made it to Festival Field.

A young policeman saluted her.

Then he bowed.

Then he took her gently by the elbow and escorted her back through the hole in the fence.

And a young man, stark naked, presented himself to the police at a back gate. He argued that he should be permitted in because he would take up less room than someone wearing clothes.

The police agreed that his argument had some validity, good reasoning behind it, but that was not the basis on which tickets had been sold. They solemnly promised they would recommend the idea to festival producers for consideration next year.

Saturday night, a young cop turned back a hot, angry and high group of about seventy by simply yawning with convincing sincerity, and saying, "Gee, kids, split, willya?"

They did.

Thus when a Volkswagen minibus rolled from somewhere onto the high ground inside Festival Field itself, it caused instant and great curiosity. How was it possible? How did it get in? No vehicles in Newport's massive gridlock had moved in more than a day. If a beautiful

148 Souvenirs of a Blown World

young woman with dignity, a naked young man with good reasoning, hadn't been permitted into Festival Field, what was this Volkswagen minibus doing here?

A man in his forties, bearded and wearing cord trousers, sort of a teacher type, got out of the Volkswagen. He ignored all the questions as to why and how he was there.

He lifted a color television onto the roof of the minibus. Inside the minibus was a silent generator.

On top of the minibus, the television flickered on.

From the hill overlooking Newport Festival Field, the stage a golden apron of light below us, bonneted with its Sister of Charity acoustic cap, Led Zeppelin's guitar live in our ears, in that incredible crowd pressed against each other as if this were our last moment on earth, we watched, on television, Man take his first step on the moon.

18 James Groppi

Religion, señor, is your own broken heart.
—Jack Kerouac

✦ ✦ ✦

"Someone punched me in the eye last night," the priest said.

High on his left cheekbone was a nasty curved cut, apparently made by a fist slamming against his glasses. The glasses he was wearing appeared to be undamaged.

"Someone else cracked me over the head with a stick. Besides that I have a terrible cold. My head is killing me."

In truth, he appeared to be going to sleep inside himself.

"Hey, Grope," one of his commandoes said. "Have you got another one of those?"

The priest snorted. "I think you can find your own beer."

"I think I can find my own beer," the kid said. "Hey, Father," he said to a young priest standing in the doorway. "You got another beer?"

That was the night Father James Groppi quit.

Every night for more than six months he had led a march from Saint Boniface Church through Milwaukee, demonstrating the need of black people for a strong fair-housing law. Every night, in heat, rain, sleet and snow the march had caused riots, street fights, mass arrests. School kids chanted, "Father Groppi's got to go! Father Groppi rest in hell!" (He said it was a tribute to their parochial education that "they call me Father"). Trucks were parked strategically along the curb to give counter-demonstrators a good rock-throwing angle. National television cameras dwelt long and frequently on the persistent little priest in Milwaukee.

Ten suburban communities passed fair-housing ordinances of varying strength and meaning as a result of his persistence.

The city of Milwaukee itself passed an ordinance which only seemed to preclude any sort of a fair-housing law ever being passed.

This was the day after his two hundredth march.

Late that afternoon, arriving late at a press conference for Father Groppi, I glimpsed the priest sagged on a stool in a small room, staring out of the shadows nervously, looking for all the world like a losing boxer waiting for the tenth-round bell.

He was thirty-eight years old, short, balding and grey complexioned. For the three summers before he had been ordained in 1959, he had directed a youth center in Milwaukee's slums. The parish of Saint Boniface was not his first assignment and was, I gathered, one he had requested.

In the white television light, Father Groppi assumed the posture before the table microphones I had seen him use in all televised press conferences: one arm over the chairback of one of his commandoes. He kept this position even when he leaned forward to answer questions heatedly.

His two commandoes were built like two middleweight boxers at full strength. One, Lawrence Friend, had been captain of commandoes and was then Chairman of the NAACP Youth Council in Milwaukee. On his blue nylon jacket was emblazoned Black and Beautiful. Wilbur Arms (the names reminded me of Andy Warhol's Paul America and Ingrid Superstar—Groppi had Friend on one side, Arms on the other) was dressed in what was described as a uniform, blue nylon jacket with a large *C* on it, a black beret. They both eye-fixated the press audience with the excessive, put-on arrogance (which they found hilarious in each other; it really broke them up) of the militant black in the forefront of the fight.

Their function was to protect church property during those troublesome times, the person of Father Groppi, and as many demonstrators as they could during a march. Neither knew how many commandoes there were.

"There are three shifts of us."

There was a reporter at the press conference who was drunk and genuinely abusive. Like the inevitable bore at the end of a Friday-night bar, he repetitiously badgered, interrupted, and straight-armed any line of questioning but his own.

His point seemed to be that a priest's function is solely spiritual, and that a priest ought not involve himself in social problems.

"The Church has been involved, as William Stringfellow says, by its noninvolvement," Father Groppi said. "I'm taking the stigma out of its noninvolvement by involving it positively. Christ was concerned with feeding the poor and the sick. . . ."

"Wait a minute, Father. Are you trying to say Christ was on a social revolution kick?"

"I do indeed. To say the Church should have nothing to do with the black equality movement is as bad as to say the Church should have had nothing to do with opposing Nazism."

"I'm not talking about Germans. Would Christ approve of marches?"

"Of course. Christ was the greatest social revolutionary who ever lived. The role of the priest today is to be involved in social reform," he said. "The main problem of the Church today is white racism."

"It's not to save souls?"

"It is to save souls. What do you mean, to save souls? When a man is a racist he is committing sin. Racism is the greatest sin against Christ because it is the sin against brotherhood."

"What do your superiors think of you?" the reporter asked.

"We've had our differences, but I'm still a functioning priest.

"Lutherans, Baptists-all have been equally guilty in being thunderous in their silence," Father Groppi said.

An hour later, Father Groppi received a standing ovation in the main ballroom of a downtown hotel.

Of the one thousand people present, a noticeable number were nuns and priests, ("There isn't much support for me from the average pulpit," Father Groppi had said. "This is a tragedy") very few black people, and a few civil rights activists (one of whom expressed surprise to me at "being in with all these people on their way to heaven").

Father Groppi came up the middle aisle slowly, flocked by his acolyte-commandoes who tried to keep people in their pew rows while the priest reached through them to shake hands. By the time he reached the front; everyone was standing, applauding.

His speech, "White Racism," was that of a tired mind trying to go in a straight line. He tried to use his own experiences as core, but had to abandon anything like chronological order.

"When I come out into white society, I known I'm on practically a different planet," he said.

"One of the reasons black militants are saying to the white man working in the ghettoes 'Get out, we don't want you anymore' is because the white person says, 'I understand.'

"No white man understands the black experience, including myself. We can grow in brotherhood, but we can never really understand."

Almost immediately after the speech began, Father Groppi's two commandoes, sitting behind him on the stage, lolled their heads and appeared to fall asleep.

"I would die for a man's right to move wherever he wants and be judged not on the color of his skin, but as a man."

He described the ghetto picture as it was in Milwaukee then. Rents were higher in the ghetto per square foot than in Whitefish Bay, Milwaukee's most prestigious address. Population in the ghetto was four times more dense than in Whitefish Bay. A recent telephone check of one hundred and four rentals advertised in a Milwaukee newspaper revealed only nine landlords would rent to blacks.

In answer to a complaint from the audience that looting is theft, he referred to Kaplovitz's book *The Poor Pay More*. "There are no price tags in those stores, you know."

He charmed the audience by telling them of his efforts to have a Black Christmas. "Black is Beautiful." He wore black vestments. He was able to find a black baby doll for the creche, but no black Mary and Joseph statues. "I admit it looked odd.

"Some find interracial marriages have developed through the youth council concept.

"I think the major problem in American cities today is the policeman," Father Groppi said. "To the whites, he is a protector. To the black community, he is the oppressor. His image is that of the occupation army. And, in most cases, they are right.

"A city like Milwaukee looks at its police department and says it can do no wrong. There's racism in the Church; you can't tell me there's not racism in the police department. Is the police department holier than the Church?

"The greatest scandal in the history of the Church is its present silence. The silence of the institutional church over real human suffering, psychological brutality is unforgivable.

"The Church should take a stand now. Windows might get broken and congregations might get smaller. But these people should be made to leave the Church. They're only passing themselves off as Christians anyway.

"We will use any tactic in the Milwaukee Youth Council we find necessary to overthrow the oppressiveness of present society.

"Please don't look at Negroes in America today and say, you are guilty of violence, when we have used it in our past and do use it today in Vietnam. That is horrid hypocrisy."

Once, when Father James Groppi was in a Milwaukee jail, a policeman asked him why he wasn't in his church with his congregation. Father Groppi pointed out that two hundred and forty-nine members of his congregation were in jail with him.

"A priest belongs with his people, wherever they may be. If they are in jail protesting social injustice, so should he be."

A Passionist priest offered three cheers to end the evening and led the audience in singing "For he's a wonderful fellow. . . ."

And we were sitting around the slum rectory dining table, trying to think of baloney and beer as food, discussing the rumors, while Father Groppi was going to sleep inside himself.

"The thing is," he said, putting down the sandwich, "I don't know what we're going to do. We're about to have a week of strategy meetings."

In that spring of 1968 the country was flooded with rumors.

First, there was the rumor that many of the leaders of the counterculture had been abroad during the winter for guerilla training in Communist countries. Some had. Their route was to Mexico City, from there to Cuba, and from there to Eastern Europe.

There was the rumor that black veterans, trained in the arts of war, very angry at their return to the United States to find themselves unemployed and unemployable, disrespected, were to be used toward violent ends by these trained leaders.

There was the rumor that the United States government had reactivated World War II prisoner-of-war camps to hold the large numbers of peace and black-equality demonstrators expected that summer.

One of Father Groppi's commandoes insisted to me he knew where such a camp was located, in northern Wisconsin near his uncle's farm. He would not say either he or his uncle actually had laid eyes on it.

Groppi's nonviolent battle for fair housing in Milwaukee appeared lost.

The backlash created appeared bigger than the gains made.

He was sick, tired and wounded.

And rumor had it that violence in this nation was to be greatly escalated in coming months.

Finally, he said, "Perhaps you could go over everything you've seen and heard since you've been with me and tell me what we're going to do next. I need to go to bed."

Leaving his beer bottle half full on the table, he excused himself.

He had his week of strategy meetings.

No announcement came from them.

Beginning that late night-early morning in March 1968, Father James Groppi faded from the news.

Ten years later, James Groppi, no longer a priest, was employed by the city of Milwaukee as a bus driver.

19 Traveling with Susi

"Mr. Mcdonald?"

"Hello?"

"This is the Republic of Ireland," crackled the lady's little voice over transatlantic telephone.

"What, all of it?"

"You've just done a series of seventy newspaper columns surveying American attitudes toward the arts, art institutions, and artists."

"True." I had run on the topic indecently. To that moment I had not known my embarrassment was international in scope.

"The point you make interests us very much. Your theme is that the United States has never passed through a period of nationalism of the sort which commits the populace to the development and dissemination of a national culture. Is that more or less correct?"

"Right on." For some reason, most of the most agreeable voices in my life have been barely audible over long-distance telephone. People who disagree with me, or think little of my work, always seem to be much closer and therefore more audible.

"We think it would be interesting for you to do a similar survey of Irish culture, as the Republic of Ireland has passed through such a period of nationalism. . . ."

Therefore, I was invited to Rosc ("Eye," a combination of national and international exhibits in the visual arts Ireland produces every four years).

I was to discover how difficult it is for the Irish to individuate themselves culturally while essentially living in the English back-yard.

I had less than a week to get ready.

I took my wife, Susi, to a consoling lunch. Again I would be traveling without her, a working tour of Ireland followed by a working stop in London. The word *working* was stressed.

At that point we had been married eight years. Our lives had been filled with our sons, working, rented quarters and second-hand cars.

We had really only traveled together once.

Shortly after we were married, a publisher determined to produce a novel of mine had us visit New York City to explain to us all that he couldn't do as a publisher.

Being newly married, I forgot to sign my wife into the hotel, a matter which, I discovered, legitimately married young ladies take seriously.

I also didn't know Susi had the peculiar habit of placing almost everything she owns in plastic sacks, which she places in brown paper bags, some of which she then places in leather sacks. Packing up, being the faithful husband, I simply put all these sacks into the car.

Which allowed Susi, standing in our room at the St. Regis Hotel, opening a few sacks in particular, to exclaim: "Why did you bring the garbage?"

When my publisher called to enquire why his young author and wife were late for cocktails, Susi blithely explained I was out taking a walk.

I was out in the alleys of New York trying to rid myself of sacks of orange peels and coffee grounds we had brought from home.

Somehow, I felt it was not the function of room service, even in such a good hotel as the St. Regis, to be met at the door and handed bags of Mcdonald garbage transported in a Ford from Massachusetts.

The mood of the consoling lunch turned mellow with existential rebellion on the parts of both of us.

Later that evening, friends volunteered to take over house and sons if Susi could accompany me.

First, I took myself to the garden for a financial discussion with myself. Traveling at other people's expense, I was to travel First Class. Susi was to travel at my expense. My arrangements could not be changed. I could not see myself visiting Susi between appointments at a crosstown boarding house. Yet First Class accommodations for Susi would put a nearly perfect bullet hole through the forehead of my bank account. Oh, what the hell.

Next, I had to ask permission of the sons.

To our dismay, they reacted with extraordinary glee. Their eyes lit up with delight at the thought of being rid of us for such a long time. Furthermore, they allowed us the impression they found our friends far more entertaining than they had ever found us anyway.

Next, I had to invite Susi.

Winning her acceptance proved remarkably easy.

She was packed that night. Not only that, but she had almost completely packed my things.

For the days before we left, I couldn't find a sock, shoe, or shirt. Everything was either at the cleaners or had been packed. It was as if I had suddenly moved somewhere else without taking me along.

I had to dress out of the furthest reaches of my closet.

It was because of this that during my absence a friend published a newspaper column, widely read, describing me as "The Best Dressed Man of 1958."

Unfortunately, it was 1971.

We were facing day after day of rough travel, which requires loose, rough clothing; day after day of meetings, which require fairly sober city clothing; night after night of formal, black-tie receptions, which are easy enough for a male, but taxing for a traveling lady.

When it became time for me to be concerned with the problem of packing, about an hour and a half before plane time, I made one of my strong speeches about not paying airplane overweight for a lot of silly, feminine clothes and, furthermore, I certainly did need to take a sweater.

Twenty minutes later, there was a shout of exultation from the bathroom. Susi addressed me from the pedestal of the bathroom scales.

"Your bag," she announced, "weighs eight pounds more than my bag."

Three times every day, including every night, Susi would be turned out differently.

However, not without first going through this feminine pleasure three times a day of standing in the middle of some hotel room, assembling herself, saying, "Is this all right? Do I look all right in this?"

At first I would look and say, "Yes, fine."

Then I stopped looking and just said, "Yes–fine."

On the fifth night, as I had other things to think about, more serious, to-the-point things, I said, "Please stop asking me that. You always look wonderful."

Shortly she appeared from the bathroom in the most ridiculous-looking thing I had ever seen in my life. I couldn't help but notice.

"You don't look wonderful," I said.

"This," she allowed me to know, "is my new slip."

"Oh."

The lady critic from *Le Figaro* burdened Susi with continuous, detailed criticism of Irish fashion.

Madame had brought no long clothes.

"We wouldn't dream of wearing such things in Paris," sniffed Madame, while continuously complimenting Susi on her foresight, her modified high style, her combinations of haute couture and young fashions which would succeed superbly in either Paris or—with a significant sniff—*Dublin*.

At each rave, Susi would give me a look which said, quite clearly, "My suitcase is eight pounds lighter than your suitcase."

Mine was a particularly heavy sweater. A great comfort to have along.

Traveling alone, I am taken as a serious American businessman, as dull as a signed contract, and thus usually left alone.

Traveling with Susi, I discovered I immediately became half of a honeymoon couple and thus included in stares from across the hotel dining room that ranged from the sweetly, comprehensibly loving to the obscenely, comprehensibly lecherous.

People introduced themselves to us by banging me on the shoulder, while I was spooning grapehit, with the line, "Just married?"

Our official driver in western Ireland, a middle-aged woman, was fastidious in her duties, but distinctly chilly.

Finally able to stand the chill from the front seat no longer, when we stopped for my eleven a.m. coffee break, I invited her to join us.

She sat in the pub with us and took a small whiskey.

"I read in the newspapers you've been married eight years?" she asked.

"We've been married eight years," Susi answered, grateful for any conversational gambit.

"Then how come you've got just the two sons?"

As I would work on the columns in the hotel rooms most mornings, Susi would go out shopping.

Go out shopping!

She was raising a riot in the land of Saint Patrick.

She discovered that every day the Number 7 bus was charging her fourpence into the center of the city and sixpence back.

She formed a caucus in the back of the bus, a coalition of housewives, grandmothers and one formidably strong ally, a priest's housekeep who could swear like a sailor, all of whom, she discovered, had been noticing this inequity for years, but doing nothing about it. The fear was general that if they questioned authority they'd be charged sixpence both ways.

Susi persuaded her followers that if a bus could go one way for fourpence, it could go the same route back for fourpence as well.

So the ladies, en masse, refused to pay the sixpence getting off.

The bus was stopped. A mammoth traffic jam ensued.

The authorities were summoned.

The ladies, vociferous in their complaint, refused to let traffic move until this injustice was solved, until the lower fare, both ways, was agreed to by the ultimate authority in Dublin in charge of buses.

The ladies won their street revolution.

Henceforth the bus went each way charging fourpence the passenger.

Her fondness for the Number 7 bus then became overweaning. It became "my bus."

One very late night, in formal wear, when we couldn't find the car that was supposed to be waiting for us, she said, "Oh, good. We'll take my bus."

"Susi, I'm sure the car will be right along."

It was cold and I was without my supper.

Of course, dressed in evening gown and black-tie, we caused stares and giggles on the Number 7 bus. These were the midnight bus riders which, in any city of the world, are apt to be people who do not expect to win any election.

The headline of the *Evening Express* being read by a man across the aisle read: Man Murdered in Dublin.

Two Blasted to Death was the headline of the newspaper further down the aisle.

From across the aisle, Susi pressed fourpence into my palm.

"It's fourpence this way now," she announced loudly, in case any of the midnight bus-riders were ignorant of the most recent reform.

The driver even made a special stop for us, right in front of the Intercontinental Hotel.

"Evening, sor," said the doorman. "Took the old Number 7, did you?"

"It's cheaper," said Susi. "And," she added significantly as she started through the swivel door, "quicker."

Susi did not restrict her good works to the public bus.

She became friends with an attractive lady named Nora O'Halpin, who had a fast car.

They took it upon themselves to buzz around consoling all the artists, one by one, whose works had not been included in any of the Rosc exhibits.

Neither understood my horror when I discovered what they were doing. All the talents who didn't get hung had to suffer the further indignity by being consoled by two ladies in a fast car!

I referred to it as their Campaign to Make Rejected Artists Absolutely Suicidal.

"They appreciate it very much," I was informed.

Checking out of the Intercontinental Hotel, Susi, victories behind her, threatened to raise another riot over the bill.

Our bills were split. The very considerable telephone bill and the very considerable laundry bill (two ways hotels commit robbery anyway) were put on her bill. In fact, she had made few telephone calls and had been doing something mysterious with her laundry.

"Why on earth do you presume that only women talk on the telephone?" was her starting explosion.

"Susi, that doesn't matter."

"And why on earth should laundry be stuck on the woman's bill? Just because it's laundry?"

"Susi, you don't understand. All that goes against a separate account."

"I do understand! Automatically they put telephones and laundry on the woman's bill! Without even thinking!"

At Brown's Hotel, in London, again we were on different schedules.

Susi took to leaving written messages for me with the hall porters, of which there always seemed to be six or seven standing around, eager to be helpful.

The hall porters, victims of British journalism, took to calling these messages *Love Lines*.

"More love lines, sir . . ."

I knew they had spent any interim, to a man, deciphering Susi's penmanship. They would flank both my shoulders, advising me of their translation, as far as they had got.

"That's an *r*, sir. Surely that's an *r*?"

"I thought we had decided that's a *b*, William?"

"A *b*, is it, Tom? Could it be a *p*?"

"The sense of it is, sir: you're late for luncheon."

"How could he be late for luncheon, George? It's just gone one o'clock."

"Because he's been late for luncheon every day this week, Anthony."

Thus gently chastised by a full hall of porters, I would then do my best to catch up with Susi.

Someone who had been usurping rather too much of my time in London, finally, guiltily, arranged theater tickets so Susi and I could spend an evening alone together.

The play we were to see was *Sleuth*.

Our seats were in the front row of the third balcony.

"I hope the play doesn't have us jumping out of our seats," said Susi, looking straight down onto the audience. "It would be fatal."

"It's called the Upper Circle, Susi."

"It's called murder," said Susi. "Won't need a sleuth to tell whodunnit."

Non-working time admittedly, I took my little book out of my jacket pocket and made a note.

"Have you been making notes on me?" Susi asked abruptly.

"How could I be?"

"Right. How could you be?"

"How could I be?" I asked, putting my notebook away.

She said, "You never listen. . . ."

20 Krishnamurti

This is why I don't like interviews. I don't feel I'm ready yet, I have the language, to control them, to say what I want without someone misquoting, distorting what I mean.

—Donovan Leitch

✦ ✦ ✦

James Klee, professor of psychology at Brandeis University, asked if I'd be interested in meeting Krishnamurti while he was on tour between the New School and Pomona. Having long been aware of the attractiveness of the Indian mystic, yet never having been able to catch precisely, concretely what he was saying that made him so attractive, I said I would indeed be interested.

Therefore I spent a Saturday morning, which was spitting rain, in Klee's office taking a cram course on the life and thought of Krishnamurti.

I was to meet with Krishnamurti before lunch.

Klee's office was twelve-feet-by-eight. It was jammed with oriental books, curios, books and ourselves.

Klee himself was six-foot-six, possessor of a considerable academic seat and a Fu Manchu beard. He sat in what can only be described as a raised throne: an enormous, upholstered, slipcovered chair on a wooden platform. "I don't fit into those other chairs," he said, directing me to one.

"The point is," he said, preparatory to introducing me to Krishnamurti, "you seem most open-minded."

Klee played for me a tape on Krishnamurti by Alan Watts. Once Episcopalian chaplain at Northwestern University, Watts then became dean of the Academy of Asian Studies in New York and then had developed a reputation as a philosophical adventurer, a writer and lecturer. His books were *The Way of Zen* and *Nature, Man and Woman*. Krishnamurti, said Watts, was someone "cut out to be a messiah, rejected that, and became an important philosopher."

Via tape recording, Watts told me the history of the Theosophical Society.

Founded in New York in 1875 by Russian emigré Madame H. P. Blavatsky and Colonel H.S. Olcott, the Theosophical Society encouraged Western belief, forever rampant anyway, in the superiority of Eastern spiritual understanding, especially the intuitive or mystical. More than that, perhaps taking advantage of the New Testament prophecy of the comforter, incited the vision of the coming of a second messiah, or the advent of the "Wise Man of the East."

Having similarities with other religious movements of the time, such as Böhmenism and the Swedenborgian, theosophy alleged knowledge of divine matters by a combination of direct mystical insight and philosophical speculation. When a series of letters Madame Blavatsky offered as divinely revelatory were proven to have been written by her own hand, she asked, "And by whose hand should they be written?"

The purposes of the Theosophical Society were to: 1) form a nucleus of a universal brotherhood of humanity without the distinctions of race, creed or color; 2) promote the study of Aryan and other Eastern literatures, religions and sciences, and demonstrate the importance of that study; and, 3) investigate unexplained laws of nature and the psychic powers latent in Man.

At the turn of the century, Madame Blavatsky and Col. Olcott journeyed to India in search of their "Wise Man of the East." Mystically enough, they found him in Madras, a babe-in-arms they could carry away and bring up themselves.

They founded, in his name, Krishnamurti, the Order of the Star of the East. The order collected vast sums of money, which was invested here and there as well as in several royal residences around the world, including Edda Castle in Holland.

Gertrude Millett, who identified herself as a member of the original Theosophical Society, having joined in 1913, wrote me that all the above information from Alan Watts, is incorrect, except for the aims of the Society. I quote from her letter: "It was Annie Besant who is responsible for Krishnamurti. Annie Besant was a member of the original society. When H.P. Blavatsky died and W.Q. Judge was made president for life, Annie Besant formed a Theosophical Society of her own which is known as the Adjar. It still exists. Later she fostered on it the idea of the coming Christ and introduced Krishnamurti."

Anyway, during the early part of this century, a little East Indian boy dressed in a tunic was dragged through Western international society as a second Christ. He was brought out every once in a while to answer profound questions with childish simplicity.

That was Krishnamurti.

In 1929, when Krishnamurti was about thirty, he renounced the movement that had been established in his name. He disbanded the worldwide Order of the Star of the East. He told the press he would "rather drive a truck than be a messiah."

He said people, to achieve a sense of spiritual and psychological security, terribly wanted an authority, and that this relinquishing of one's own authority was a kind of slavery. He took to answering questions like Is there a God? with answers like Why do you want to know?

Arriving intuitively at the point of many intellectual and philosophical discussions which had taken place the previous century, Krishnamurti announced that by adopting faiths and beliefs, Man was only protecting himself and denying his natural openness to existence and essence.

The difficulty is that, unlike more disciplined philosophers who had preceded him, whom he had not read ("I do not read books," he was to tell me—coming into his presence I was to discover him reading *Time* magazine), the truth of any intuitive conclusion of his therefore requires faith.

Certainly he phrased this contention as an unproven, unprovable absolute.

Although he renounced his messiahship, in the subsequent forty years he did not lose his following among Theosophists. Apparently they took his renunciation as an act of humility, self-denial, not only compatible with but necessary to being a messiah.

Klee told me that every place Krishnamurti lectured during those forty years (he never did drive a truck) he had to remain courteous to the hordes of original followers, now white-haired ladies who always overflow the hall.

Four books Klee lent me, gathered (edited by D. Rajagopal) from Krishnamurti's lectures and interviews, *Commentaries on Living* (First, Second and Third Series), plus *Life Ahead*, were all published by Quest Books, a division of the Theosophical Society in America.

To simple questions in the books are offered long allegories, which one can occasionally find relevant, but only by intellectual backbends. In my search for an explicit answer to an explicit question, I found that to the question, Why can we not be free of disease and death? Krishnamurti answered, Why are you so preoccupied with it? . . . Death is merely the extinction of continuity, and we are afraid of not being able to continue; but what continues can never be creative. Ah, well, to continue, one way or the other. . . .

Klee attested the thoughts of Krishnamurti figured prominently in mind expansion then much in vogue.

Alan Watts said, "No one interested in the impact of Eastern thought upon the West can afford . . . to overlook . . . Krishnamurti."

Watts also referred to Krishnamurti as "the philosopher of nothing in particular."

✦ ✦ ✦

So, in two cars, Klee and I went through the rain to a nearby motel to meet the retired Star of the East.

We were met in the motel driveway by Krishnamurti's secretary, Alan Naude, a man in his forties, a retired pianist, he said, in a high-waisted blue blazer.

Going down the motel corridor to Krisnamurti's room, we were followed by a puppy.

"I have never seen Krishnamurti," said Klee, "that a dog has not been mysteriously and unusually present."

"A dog or a baby," said Naude. "There always seems to be a dog or a baby."

This particular dog stopped outside someone else's door to clean off a breakfast tray left on the floor.

Putting down *Time* magazine, Krishnamurti rose in silent greeting.

Klee directed immediate attention to a stopwatch propped against Krishnamurti's bureau mirror.

"I use it to time my breathing exercises," said Krishnamurti.

He demonstrated how he breathes.

While Naude sat on the edge of one bed like a pianist about to strike an opening chord, Klee sat in one of those chairs into which he did not fit.

I sat in a chair near the window.

Krishnamurti sat on the far edge of the nearer bed.

During the course of what I had meant to be an interview, Krishnamurti went across his bed somehow, up the nearer edge, and took my hand, and held it. Which is not something many of the people I interviewed did, as, among other things, it hampers note taking.

In his speaking to me, Krishnamurti made sweeping and inaccurate presumptions about me. He presumed I had absolute religious and political points of view, and was happy with neither. He also presumed I had unhappy points of view regarding my wife, my children, my business, my life in general.

Being unhappy has always struck me as an unworthy and tiresome self-indulgence.

Krishnamurti asked a question, presumptuously, as if from my own lips, and then set about answering it. Controlling the conversation indeed. He debated, apparently between himself and me, while I remained a silent witness.

With annoyance at having myself so badly represented in this duologue, as well as with desire to get the interview moving in some direction, I decided to step in on my side of the discussion and, if not supply the question, at least supply the answer.

"You abominate violence, right?"

"No. At times I believe it most appropriate."

"You do not abominate violence? You do not abominate conflict?"

"Conflict can be wonderfully healthy."

"Conflict is sickness," he corrected me. "How can you say conflict is healthy?"

"How can you have growth without conflict?"

"That is the point. All that—change, movement, growth—is an illusion."

"Then how can I agree with you?"

It was at that early moment that Naude's feet began looking uselessly for the piano pedals on the rug.

Krishnamurti was saying that one should be observing without ever making an observation.

"The moment you measure, you are bringing to it the intellectual capacity of comparison, conclusion, and a state of mind that is not free results."

While I examined Krishnamurti's monogrammed shirt, customtailored with full sleeves and an oversized collar, I supposed to accentuate his slightness, I listened to him debate with himself ideas not new to me, and not particularly Eastern.

It was not his point, he said, that one is bound to act in accordance with one's conclusions, as much as it was that one should not conclude, so that one cannot act. Action is illusion.

"Ideologies, which are conclusions, have separated human beings into Communists, Catholics, Protestants, and causes wars and all that."

One should bring nothing from the past, he told me, in looking at anything, but should see it freshly, without the obstruction of memory.

One should also bring no consideration of the future in contemplating the present. One, for example, should not consider the ultimate demise of anyone with whom one hopes to relate directly.

"You see that oak tree through the window?" he asked.

I did not look, as I had never seen Krishnamurti before.

"You can only see that tree, see it at all as itself, if you can see it absolutely without knowledge, without memory of other trees, without comparison with other trees."

I was obliged to give him the essentential answer to the existential question: "Then why did you refer to it as an *oak* tree? Why do you refer to it as *a tree* at all?"

Jumping up, Alan Naude declared it time for lunch.

The puppy was scratching at the door.

✦ ✦ ✦

"It was interesting understanding what Krishnamurti is saying," I said to James Klee over our own lunch.

"You do understand."

"The nihilism that was buried in the rubble of Berlin in 1945 permitted people deliberately, consciously to act evil. The nihilism Krishnamurti is preaching does not permit people to act at all."

"Action is illusion," he quoted.

After lunch we found a long line of young people standing in the spitting rain, quietly awaiting a two- or three-minute personal interview with Krishnamurti.

They were waiting to talk with someone who would tell them nothing.

21 Three Ladies of the Theatre: Swanson, Stapleton, Grenfell

Action is illusion.

—Krishnamurti

✦ ✦ ✦

When a long, black limo slips up to your door on a twelve-thirty Tuesday noon and there is in the backseat a superstar of Gloria Swanson's luminosity, wrapped in fur, to take you to her hotel suite, one might reasonably presume lunch. Especially after a comparatively thin Monday and a Tuesday that thus far had produced very little in the edible line.

On the way to her place she talked of reviews of her play, *Butterflies Are Free*, which had opened the night before. That the other female in the cast had been mentioned in the reviews appeared to disturb her.

On the table in her living room there was a splendid basket of fresh fruit.

"Go ahead," Gloria Swanson said. "Have a banana. They're poisoned. They've all been sprayed. I'm going to change."

I did not have a banana.

The night before, at the opening-night cast party, she had looked along the cold buffet with disdain, and deigned not.

She had said to me: "Today is the day I think I shall have a cigarette."

We were all very interested in that.

After her first puff, a member of her entourage came along, took the cigarette from her, and crushed it out.

Later, a more sympathetic member of her entourage said, "She's been saying she would have a cigarette for weeks."

"That was it?"

"I guess so."

At twelve-twenty-two midnight after her play had opened, Gloria Swanson momentarily drew smoke.

She reentered the living room in a pantsuit, soft leather, size two-and-a-half boots and a long, white grace coat.

From her corner of the divan, she said, making a face, "Would you prefer a hard drink, or . . ." actually sticking her tongue out with repulsion, ". . . a soft drink?"

"Uh, gee, no, thanks, Miss Swanson. Guess I'll pass that up."

A glass of mountain water was gotten me from the kitchen. One was to drink it at room temperature. The ice, not being made of mountain water, was poisonous. In her kitchen, Miss Swanson had twelve cases of mountain water.

It was real good water.

"You may have a sandwich," she said reluctantly.

"Oh, no, thanks."

I knew I couldn't stand the faces while I ate.

We sat next to each other on the divan, in clear sight of the bowl of fruit.

In 1913, at the age of fourteen years and six months, Miss Swanson began working as an extra at the Essanay Studio in Chicago. Her first starring role was in George Ade's *Elvira, Farina and The Meal Ticket.*

"I can tell you about a doctor," Gloria Swanson began, "who came to apologize because I was having dinner there and there were about seventeen persons there and I always bring my own food to dinner and eat it upstairs so people don't ask about it, but I came down to the kitchen for a fork and met the doctor and he said, 'Look. Have a peach. Aren't they beautiful?'

"I said, 'I want to stick it in my stomach, not my eye. You should be ashamed of yourself you—a doctor—offering food that has been sprayed.'"

One month shy of seventeen, Miss Swanson, an army brat, arrived with her mother in Hollywood.

Although she was in a Mack Sennett picture, for years she denied, rightly, she had ever been a "Mack Sennett Bathing Beauty."

She made six pictures for Cecil B. DeMille before 1921, twenty-one for Paramount before 1925, seven for her own production company between 1927 and 1934 (she had rather a "come back" under the aegis of her own production company in 1928), one for Fox in 1934 and another for RKO in 1941. Miss Swanson's next and last picture, then, was *Sunset Boulevard* in 1949.

"An orange is picked," Miss Swanson continued. "It is like yanking a child out of a womb. It's picked off the tree while it's still trying to be an orange. It's green. Men are too greedy to leave that orange alone."

Miss Swanson thinks of herself as an orange, I wrote on my notepad.

"They have to gas an orange that way to make it orange. Crooked nonsense. Just to make a buck."

Miss Swanson also made a picture, *Queen Kelly*, produced by Joseph P. Kennedy, the father of the late president, in 1928, which has never been shown theatrically. The Museum of Modern Art in New York has a print of this film, and occasionally schedules a showing.

Although Miss Swanson has three children, Gloria, Joseph and Michelle, Joseph is the only one of the three who is adopted. In years, he is the middle child.

I meant to ask Miss Swanson about that, over a quiet lunch.

"In America, you can call anything on a plate 'food.' If there's a big enough pile of it and chocolate sauce on it, it could be you know what."

"I've been on a high protein diet since I was born," I said defensively.

"Meat is pretty sick in this country. Why else do they give them antibiotics. And then female sex hormones to make them fatter.

"Once, a mink grower discovered that when he fed the mink chicken heads shot with female sex hormones, the mink would be sterile in six months."

"I haven't had that problem yet," I put in.

At seventy-two, Miss Swanson retained the marvelous nose, the huge blue eyes, the magnificent cheeks that seemed to enlarge like glass blown with light when she laughed.

"I'll tell you how I started on this food business," she said, at ten minutes past two. "It was in 1928 and I was being a movie producer and therefore thought I had to have an ulcer, so I went to this doctor, Dr. Harry Bieler, Hal Bieler, of whom I since became a disciple, although he should have been dead years ago, poor dear.

"Well, he sat me down and took a big piece of foolscap and a pencil and said, 'Now, Miss Swanson, I want you to tell me everything you had for dinner last night.'

"And I said, 'Oh, the usual things. Meat and potato,' and he said, 'No, that was what you had at table. What did you have before you ever got to the table?'

"So I said, 'Some Drambuie, no gin in it. Some olives, wrapped in bacon.' He was taking it all down on his pad. At table I told him I had some shrimp with a condiment sauce, then an oxtail soup with sherry on the side. . . .'"

Besides her apartment on Fifth Avenue, Miss Swanson had an estate in Palm Springs, and a house in Portugal.

". . . a white fish with almonds, a white wine, a bird with a separate wine . . . a salad, with Thousand Island dressing, asparagus with a Hollandaise sauce . . ."

Attorney General Robert Kennedy and President John F. Kennedy chat in
White House doorway in 1963. *(Reprinted courtesy Associated Press Newsfeatures)*

Self portrait: Jack Kerouac.
(Printed courtesy Gregory Mcdonald Collection, 20th Century Archives)

United States Army Private First Class Claude Smith, 1966. *(Reprinted courtesy* Boston Globe, *staff photograph)*

Actor John Wayne.
*(Reprinted courtesy
U.P.I.—Bettman
Archives)*

Ralph Schoenman, Secretary
to Lord Bertrand Russell.
(Reprinted courtesy Boston
Globe*; staff photograph)*

Entertainer Tiny Tim, 1968. *(Courtesy Gifford/Wallace, Inc.)*

Gregory Mcdonald and Andy Warhol, 1966. In background is Warhol's Marilyn Monroe silkscreen. *(Reprinted courtesy* Boston Globe*; Gilbert Friedberg photograph)*

Actor Rock Hudson, 1971.
(Courtesy M.G.M.)

Poet Hugh MacDiarmid and Gregory Mcdonald, 1967.
(Reprinted courtesy Boston Globe*; staff photograph)*

Singer Joan Baez, 1972. *(Courtesy M. A. Greenhill)*

Singer, composer Donovan Leitch, 1967. *(Photo by Stephen A. Hansen)*

Director Tom O'Horgan, 1968.
(Reprinted courtesy Boston Globe*; staff photograph)*

Father James Groppi in Dane County
Jail cell after being arrested for contempt
of Wisconsin State Assembly, 1969.
*(Reprinted courtesy
Associated Press Wirephoto)*

Philosopher Krishnamurti. *(Reprinted courtesy* Boston Globe*; staff photograph)*

Actress Gloria Swanson, onstage in "Butterflies Are Free," 1971.
(Reprinted courtesy Boston Globe; *staff photograph)*

Singer, composer Phil Ochs, 1968. *(Photo by Steven A. Hansen)*

Designer L. Francis Herreshoff, 1967, outside his baronial house in Gloucester, Massachusetts. *(Reprinted courtesy* Boston Globe; *Gilbert Friedberg photograph)*

Sculptor Louise Nevelson, 1965. *(Photo by Diana Mackown)*

Abbie Hoffman having his hair shorn in front of Federal Building during Chicago Conspiracy Trial. He sent hair to Jerry Rubin, in jail, "to give Jerry strength." *(Reprinted courtesy U.P.I.—Bettman Archives)*

Original October 14, 1970. United Press International caption on this photo read: "President Nixon sniffs a package of marijuana, at the White House 10/14, during a Customs Bureau demonstration on how dogs can detect hidden drugs." *(Reprinted courtesy U.P.I.—Telephoto-Bettman Archives)*

Gregory Mcdonald, 1970. *(Photo by Charles Martin, Jr.)*

"This is all very interesting," I said to Miss Swanson at two-twenty-three.

". . . for dessert, a trifle, with champagne . . ."

"Miss Swanson, do you ever get hungry? Even a teensy bit? I mean, like, say, around two-thirty on Tuesday afternoons. I mean, just like, for example, I mean?"

She continued: "And the doctor said, 'Fine. Now what I want you to do is close your eyes . . .'" Miss Swanson waited for me to close my eyes, "'and envision all that food, the pig, the fish, the bird, the sauces and salads, dumped upside down in a pail.'"

She waited for my reaction.

"Ah," I said.

And then I said, "Ah."

Fully aware that it is rude to repeat oneself, even when not at table, I rounded up with: "Ah."

Miss Swanson had divorced five husbands: Wallace Beery, Herbert Somborn, Marquis de la Falaise de la Coudray, Michael Farmer, and William Davey.

They might have wanted lunch.

✦ ✦ ✦

With a bottle of champagne I caught Maureen Stapleton in New York while she was filming *Plaza Suite* while simultaneously rehearsing *The Gingerbread Lady* for Broadway. Both works are by Neil Simon.

I mentioned to her that Neil Simon had told me he had written the lead of *Gingerbread Lady* especially for her.

"He did? He never told me that.

"He's romanticizing!

"Let me put it this way. If I should drop dead over this champagne, he'd find, someone else to open the play!"

In 1943, at the age of eighteen, Maureen Stapleton went to New York with one hundred dollars she had earned working in a munitions factory in Troy, New York. She wanted to be an actress. She became a night billing clerk at the Hotel New Yorker.

She spent her days studying with Herbert Berghof, then at the New School for Social Research. She was in the first class at Actors Studio, with Montgomery Clift, Marlon Brando, Eli Wallach and David Wayne.

Her Broadway debut was in 1946, in the revival of *The Playboy of the Western World*. Then *Antony and Cleopatra, Detective Story, The Bird Cage*, and, the role that made her a star, Serafina Delle Rose in *The Rose Tattoo* in 1951.

Neil Simon had referred to Maureen Stapleton in print as "the best actress in America, and one of the best actresses in the world." To me, there is no actress in the world who uses her legs to act, better than Maureen Stapleton.

"I'm forty-five and I'm tired. Let me be honest. I'd rather do movies. You do it, you go home, and you're done.

"It's in your mind, with a movie, I can do it again.

"But once the curtain is up, you're on that train of performance until eleven o'clock.

"Frankly, I want to retire.

"Why didn't some rich man love me?

"I keep thinking someone rich is going to meet me at the stage door some night and say, 'Let me take you away from all this!'

"In two minutes, I'd tell Doc Simon where to shove his cookies."

When you lit a cigarette for Miss Stapleton, she held your match hand in both her hands, inhaled and looked into your eyes. One hoped that she, at least, would never give up smoking.

"Are you rich?" she asked. "Will you marry me?"

"Let me take you away from all this!" I said.

"I'm an Irish peasant," she said sadly, looking into her champagne. "With expensive tastes."

◆ ◆ ◆

We were sitting in the living room of Joyce Grenfell's cozy Chelsea flat. My old friend, the greatest English monologist and character actress, was pouring tea. Her husband, Reggie, was in Africa, where he had to go three or four times a year on business. They were married when Joyce was nineteen and they were soon to celebrate their forty-third wedding anniversary. Another old, respected friend, Virginia Graham Thesiger, widowed from one of the world's most marvelous men since I had last seen her, was unable to attend. So it was just Joyce and my wife and myself at tea. Although I had known Joyce thirteen years, this was the ladies' first meeting.

Oh, we had a lot to talk about. Joyce's mother was a Virginian, and an ancestor was Sargent, and Sargent's portrait of her grandmother hung over a desk to my left. Joyce began as a journalist, and I thanked her for two or three pieces of advice she had given me years before, on things in general, which advice I had not only followed assiduously but passed on with, I'm sure, a fearful mixture of pride and pomposity.

"You were very advanced for your time, if I remember correctly," Joyce Grenfell said over the teapot. "You wore blue jeans in London."

Joyce Grenfell was then on tour. The night before she had drawn an audience of two thousand eight hundred in Manchester's largest, the Royal Theater, which had a seating capacity of two thousand five hundred ("Three hundred people stood up for me last night—something you've never done") and she was finishing her tour in London the next night. She had sold out three weeks in advance, within two days of first notice. And sometime that week she was to videotape four half-hour television programs for the British Broadcasting Company.

We appreciated, very much, her giving us tea.

I was slightly worried, however, because Joyce Grenfell was getting much better looking as she matured. And that is not especially good for a character actress—monologist.

"Nonsense," she said at my complaint. "It's just that you're getting older, my dear. Give me another ten years and you'll think I'm a raving beauty."

Then her lovely extending of a plate with her hand, looking at me like a horse. "Bisquit?"

I feel inadequate in place of an audience of two thousand eight hundred. Nevertheless, I hazarded a question as to what comprised her one-woman show on that particular tour.

Suddenly, she was many things, many people, an old London street woman singing a sentimental song for a theater queue while she can't quite keep her false teeth in, a remarkable, well-read, two hundred—pound African driver (she met through her husband, Reggie) reciting Browning, a royal dowager opening "the new wing" of a building "for the good of the people," a Southern belle (which accent she had from her mother) explaining why she can't come to the ball. All at once, lightning snatches of personalities and songs, a few serious, ending with the dame singing a recital who suddenly remembers she left the stove on at home and into whose lyrics creep unconscious, worried references to eggs, puddings and scalded pots, as well as husband's rage.

My mind flipped back to the days when she used to dig a skinny American kid out of his cold rooms for Sunday dinner, "a genuine, home-cooked, feed up, or whatever you call it"; then sitting at table with Joyce and Reggie while we all discovered that Sunday dinner, although home-cooked, was no feed up, again, as Joyce was no better a cook than you would expect, and Joyce becoming increasingly entertaining at her end of the table, Reggie becoming increasingly dour and morose at his, forking the rubbery chicken, the elastic pudding, while I, in the middle, would be laughing so hard I couldn't eat a thing. Joyce's were the greatest dinners in the world. At the end, your stomach would still be empty, but your sides would be splitting.

And here, Susi and I were rollicking on the couch.

There was a telephone call, during which we couldn't help discovering Joyce had her whole, incredible schedule in her head, minute-for-minute, for weeks in advance. No "See my lawyer, agent, dressmaker, accountant" from her.

"Thematically," I put forward, "you are still advocating individuality."

"Of course," she said. "Which is why you and I are such good friends. Nothing much interests us but the individual."

"I do hope your wife can stand us."

"She's an individual."

"Seriously," she said, putting down her teacup. "I've never had trouble attracting an audience, but they keep putting me in bigger and bigger halls, and more and more people come. I appear on television and ratings leap. It must mean something.

"I do espouse the individual above all other things, and, as you well know, I do believe that things ultimately make sense.

"I guess people sense these things from me, as you did a long time ago, and apparently we have come to an era in which people need these things, desperately.

"Individuality. The sacredness of the character, without this nasty, putting-down kind of nihilism that has been so much in vogue in recent years.

"It's so exciting, having people so perceptive of what you're doing, so appreciative and warm."

"Are you doing any films?"

"No. Half those offered me are identical to all the films I used to do, and the other half I wouldn't be seen going to, let alone in.

"Now, enough of this professional talk. First, I want to see snapshots of your sons, then I have some new paintings to show you, and you haven't even been in the study yet, where I used to scold you unmercifully, yes, the piano in there is the same, the same old spinet you used to say clunked. . . ."

22 Phil Ochs

Chaos is what is.

—Joan Baez

✦ ✦ ✦

He had just finished a two-hour solo concert and a half-hour tape interview with a college radio station and he was really keyed-up and exhausted so we went for a sandwich–beer. He had left LA that morning and was going back the next and therefore on the East Coast had a screwed-up time sense and the sandwich–beer turned into a salad–sandwich–various drinks celebration. In those first weeks after its release everything turned into a celebration because *Pleasures of the Harbor* (A&M Records) is so beautiful wonderful great, not just another record, not even to him. It sold fifty-five thousand copies in its first weeks, which for him was really beautiful wonderful great.

"There has never been a record like this," Phil Ochs said. "This is the first of its kind, you see, because it's scored like a movie. Each song is a different scene. Each song hits the ears of a different age group."

Music had been written for the violin, for the piano, for voice, the chamber ensemble, the chorus, the symphony orchestra, for the stage, and all these forms, without exception, even opera and other musicals, had been adapted to the record. From the ballad or other popular piece that will not go, reliably, beyond three and a half minutes for airplay (so not too great a time will lapse between commercials, lest you forget your primary function is as a consumer, not as a listener), to the collection of alike pieces ("We need one more baroque trumpet piece by Anon. for Side Two, Charley"), to music distilled, edited down to balance the sides of a long-playing album (Ethel Merman in a hurry), to enormous, multirecord packages wherein a symphony might spread over two and a half sides (the first movement of *Eroica* on one side, the second, third and fourth movements of Symphony No. 4 in B-flat Major on the reverse side) were adapted to the record.

But no music, until Phil Ochs, was ever written for the recording as a form in-and-of itself.

Oh, sure, there were the "let's make a record" records of the 1930s and 40s and 50s and we all heard the music, music, music sitting under the apple tree with no one else but you in the harbor lights. But these short forms were limited really by the amount of time allotted songs on the radio, rather than by seventy-eight revolutions per minute. It was shocking, in the 1960s, to have radio so diminished that the biggest singing stars, Frank Sinatra, Elvis Presley and Englebert Humperdinck (don't forget that name), dared go beyond their three and a half minutes, wailing that my way had resulted in leaving the cake out in the rain (and I'm not sure I'll be able to bake it again), even though *the record* had been traveling at forty-five and thirty-three revolutions per minute for years.

People were still performing live in New York, Las Vegas, Chicago, Los Angeles. Making a record, getting it played on the air, getting it on the Hit Parade, the Top Forty, was one's strongest negotiating tool in working out a concert tour contract.

The record business exploded. Radio airplay was still important to sell the records (although in many cases, being denied airplay during that revolutionary era resulted in more sales, e.g., *Jesus Christ Superstar*, which was denied airplay for two years, was taken as a cause and finally did very well commercially. It also resulted in a booming FM-radio business, administrators of which frequently cozzened revolutionary attitudes themselves and were looking for music not being played on AM stations. But instead of hit records being a negotiating wedge for concert tour contracts, the business really flipped and the tour became simply a device to sell records. ("You're not selling well in the midwest, Spider. See if you can get booked into the Cow Palace.")

Simply the news that someone was going to perform in an area triggered record sales. All the kids wanted to be up for the concert.

It is little wonder so few performers actually showed up for their performances. Or, that when they did show up, their performances were so shoddy.

You might have been impressed by the five, ten, fifteen thousand dollars performers were supposed to get paid for such appearances. Mere peanuts. Hardly worth coming down for, getting up for, when you realize the figures of record sales. Such became so great that established performers even stopped going through the motions of pretending they were going on tour.

The record, the LP, the *album* became more important financially, than any other thing—airplay; appearing on television; making a movie. An investment of five to fifty thousand dollars (most of which would be for publicity of one sort or another) could gross three to five million dollars in a matter of months. "Gee," said the girl to Arlo Guthrie in the movie, *Alice's Restaurant*, "someday you're going to be an album!"

The record itself became important and "writing for the record"— an integrated, long-playing album with a central theme, cohesive, coherent, comprehensive, with a single perspective, with an internal complement, melodically, rhythmically—became a short, logical hop which no one at first made. It sort of just happened. Guthrie's *Alice's Restaurant*, which was originally one side of an album, and the Beatles' *Sgt. Pepper's Lonely Hearts Club Band* indicated the trend. Ochs's *Pleasures of the Harbor* was the conscious, deliberate, well-thought-out breakthrough. It was followed by Peter Townsend's rock opera, *Tommy* and Neil Diamond's *Tap Roots Manuscript—African Trilogy*.

And these remain the most notable musical works, in their genre, of the age.

Of vast importance was the element of sound effects possible when writing for the record rather than for the concert hall. A French horn, not feasible economically on tour, or even a full chorus, can be written in for just eight bars without obligation on the part of the composer to use them ever again. Sixteen bars on a Moog synthesizer; the scream of a subway, the whine of a jet.

Writing with the long-playing record as the object, not the radio, not the concert hall, the movie or television, was first conceived and accomplished by Phil Ochs, who hitherto had a reputation as one more not wonderfully talented political polemicist folksinger.

Pleasures of the Harbor is beautiful wonderful great because it makes a complete, literate social comment such as people seldom make, which you can sit and listen to while evidence of its accuracy relentlessly passes by your nose.

Listen:

We had walked around this corner near the concert hall to go into this bar/restaurant and three cops were strung across the sidewalk obstructing traffic, gossiping, and they saw us coming and decidedly stayed in our way because we were only citizens, see. And the two cops sitting in the patrol wagon at the curb set off their siren at Karen who was with us in the eleven o'clock night and wriggled their eyebrows at the cops on the sidewalk who wriggled their eyebrows at Karen but did not move because they were cops, see.

Oh, look outside the window
There's a woman being dragged
They've dragged her to the bushes
And now she being stabbed.
Maybe we should call the cops and try to stop the pain
But Monopoly is so much fun I'd hate to blow the game.

In the restaurant the hostess turned her head to us and her face was a death mask of Twiggy. She asked if we were eating or just drinking. The four of us could not have one of the tables if we were just drinking, she said. So we ordered sandwiches and drinks at the table and all the waitress brought us for a long time were drinks.

> Smoking marijuana is more fun than drinking beer
> But a friend of ours was captured and they gave him thirty year.
> Maybe we should raise our voices, ask somebody why.
> But demonstrations are a drag, besides we're much too high.

Which record as a single began to go in LA until the Federal Communications Commission called the station and told them not to play it again. "And I'm sure it wouldn't interest anybody" (it's called: "Outside of a small circle of friends").

"The main thing I do is songwriting. There is always the question, how much can a song do? politically or any other way." The piped music in the restaurant was "Love Is Blue," over and over again. "This is what I spend my time thinking about."

He wrote:

> I'm going to give
> All that I've got to give
> Cross my heart
> And I hope to live.

Phil Ochs was born in El Paso, Texas, December 19, 1940. His daddy was a doc of Polish descent; his mother a Scottish lady immigrant. He went to high school in Columbus, Ohio, where the family had moved when he was about twelve.

"As soon as Elvis Presley came along I turned on the radio and left it on. Then I found Hank Williams and Pete Seeger."

He graduated from the Stanton Military Academy in Virginia. After three years studying journalism he went home from the campus of Ohio State to tell his apolitical parents the college administration was pecking down on him for his songs and pro-Castro editorials he was writing in his own newspaper, *The Word*, and that he was dropping out to hit the road as a folksinger.

"Up until the Cuban invasion I had been sort of moderate left," Phil said over his own half bottle of wine. "It was that incident, the Bay of Pigs, that convinced me there was a lot of political fraud going on. So I sat down and wrote 'The Ballad of the Cuban Invasion.' It was never recorded. But I realized what I was to do."

In 1961, his mother said, "It's next to impossible to make it in show business. It's stupid to saddle yourself with politics, too."

The first place he sang professionally was Farrager's in Cleveland, in 1962. Farrager's Club was also famous as the starting point for the Smothers Brothers, a comedy team whose career rose terribly fast to a weekly national television program, which was summarily cancelled by the network as a result of pressure brought by advertisers, listeners, and individual network stations, because of its political comment.

"I went to New York and met Bob Dylan before he had made it really big, and of course he was doing the same thing, only more poetically. Then there were six or seven guys in Greenwich Village all doing the same thing. It was sort of a school, only we weren't that close. We'd all come out of the Midwest and liked Elvis Presley and wanted to write about the world as it is, you know, write about the news."

Ochs's first two albums were called *All the News That's Fit to Sing* and *I Ain't Marchin' Any More*. His songs, almost without exception, were purely political protest songs.

"A key myth of America is the solo figure with a guitar. Hank Williams, Johnny Cash and Presley are the key to American music. It's the true American form, the singing cowboy. It will go on as long as the country will. That's why, no matter what my records do, I'll be alone on stage with my guitar. What I am is Elvis Presley, with a message."

His style was really weird, the way the world goes.

Ochs had three agents working for him at once, one of whom was his brother, Mike, none of whom seemed to do him any good because no one ever knew where Phil Ochs was (he's alone somewhere on an airplane with his guitar . . . of course we don't know his schedule . . . no one's with him . . .). He would show up at concerts dragging his own guitar case through the lobby because there was never anyone to show him the stage door, apologize to the ticket-taker for not having a ticket, excuse the guitar case, explain it and thus himself, wander through the theater, backstage, then on.

He would lumber back and forth behind the microphones, shuffling his feet like a schoolboy called on to recite, looking at the audience reluctantly, shyly. His face would seem more preoccupied in trying to remember his own words than in creating any sort of mood. He wore stove-pipe workpants, sincerely dusty boots, a straight leather jacket, as a country workman really would wear, and Christmas green or red shirts open at the throat. He referred to his clothes as "sort-of-natural-on-purpose Presley." And he worked at putting across a song the way a man in those clothes would work at anything, felling trees or grading roads.

The waitress said: "You have to order another drink now. State law. You can't order after one o'clock."

I saw Phil Ochs once go through an entire concert without making a single comment about the microphones not being on. He just worked hard to fill the twelve-hundred-seat hall, nearly filled, with his own lungs. He refrained from reacting at all when the mikes were turned on the last four minutes of his concert. He sang two encores, posed for some silly fraternity pictures, talked with a couple-dozen kids for an hour with a hoarse voice about Bob Dylan's latest record. He never said a word of complaint to anyone. Later, privately, he said: "Yeah, damn."

The waitress brought us more drinks. "You have to drink up. All drinks must be off the table by one-fifteen."

Phil Ochs said: "I've always felt very American. When I was twenty-one I felt I had a one-to-one relationship with this country. Kennedy had his faults, but he was heading this country away from madness. Everything that has happened since the death of Kennedy, the whole history of this country, day-by-day, has been blacker and blacker, more and more insane.

"I said to myself, if they use the nuclear bomb in Vietnam, I just won't feel like an American anymore. Then I asked myself, What are they doing now, in using napalm? It's been a steady process of numbing, of alienation.

"I believe in a real America."

The Party
The hostess is enormous
She fills the room with perfume
She meets the guests
And smothers them with greeting
And she asks How are you?
And she offers them a drink
The countess of the social grace
Who never seems to blink
And she promises to talk to you
If you promise not to think.

The restaurant hostess came by and said drinks had to be off the table by one-fifteen. She splashed the rest of Karen's drink into her glass and took photographer Steve Hansen's empty milk glass.

Phil Ochs was saying, "This country hasn't abolished free speech. It's just made free speech useless. Spock can speak today because speaking today is totally ineffectual. And they know it."

A third waitress came by and noticed we weren't drinking.

"All drinks have to be off the table by one-fifteen," she said. "Drink up."

"I have three albums on the Elektra label," Phil Ochs said, "and they're all superpolitical. The concert album, three years ago, is most important. A very explicit, exact statement of where the country was heading. And it proved to be right. I was positive it would happen big, but it didn't. Which is the main reason why I left Elektra."

Karen was giving our original waitress our water glasses.

"So I took time before the new record, *Pleasures of the Harbor*. I had a superstrong conception of an album as a complete, unified, integrated thing, like a movie. From song to song the scene shifts from scene to scene. Like the climax of the album is 'Crucifixion,' about John Kennedy's death, and it comes just after the lyric qualities of the 'Pleasures of the Harbor' piece."

"Drink up, drink up," the hostess said.

"And I wanted it to appeal to the ears of all ages. So I backed each piece with orchestration familiar to a specific group. There is classical, ragtime, 1930s cocktail music, so forth, something different behind each song. *Harbor* tries to get all time scales, hit the ears of every generation."

As a matter of fact, in putting together the separate pieces, Phil Ochs hired the most famous musicians of the various musical eras and genres, (some of whom hadn't worked in years, ever since their music went out of style) so the background would sound authentic to the generation familiar with them.

"When I was all ready, had everything written and programmed, I went with it to A&M, which has the best production, technical people. I even got Larry Marks, who is interested in scoring movies, to score this album."

Listen:

The restaurant hostess picked up Phil Ochs's glass of wine and tipped his head back enough to pour it down his throat.

"You've been talking since you came in here," she said.

While he was spluttering, she filled his glass again.

Another waitress, a blonde in her sixties, was stroking the back of my neck and the right side of my face, for some reason of her own.

> Her name's Miranda
> She's a Rudolph Valentino fan
> And she doesn't claim to understand
> She makes brownies for the boys in the band.
> —"Miranda"

"Drinks have to be off the table?" Phil Ochs asked.

He took the full glass of wine from the hostess and slid off his seat and sat under the table to finish it, laughing hilariously at his joke, at the world which day-by-day had been getting blacker and blacker, more and more insane.

> And my shoulders had to shrug
> As I crawled beneath the rug
> And retuned my piano.
> —"The Party"

After the laugh, he returned to his seat and, showing all the un-Presley, military academy, stone-sober, son of an Ohio G.P. breeding and dignity, handed the hostess the wineglass with precisely one swallow left in it. And by a look, by a gesture, made her retreat with it.

It was one-seventeen. We split.

Stepping around the cops on the sidewalk, heading for the cab, Phil Ochs said, "This album is very peculiar. Phil Ochs, the protest singer, could have made a folk-rock record. The lyrics are good. If I had made a folk-rock record of these lyrics, it would have even been more of an instant hit. I didn't. This doesn't fit into the pop mold. For a reason. I believe *Pleasures of the Harbor* has to carve its own space. It doesn't fit into any category you can name. Yet. It has to be good enough on its own. You can't like it because it fits into a category. I wanted a record that makes sense unto itself, unto its own lyrics. Therein lies its strength, and its weakness.

"And if that is true, then it will never die."

Within minutes then, it seemed, only a year or two, Phil Ochs was dead, of misadventure.

> I'm going to give
> All that I've got to give
> Cross my heart
> And I hope to live.

23 The Opiate of the People

Obladi, oblada, life goes on, bra.
—The Beatles

✦ ✦ ✦

"Do you mean to say the man who got you pregnant isn't respectable?"
"Yes. It's Miguel Garcia."
". . . No wonder she wouldn't tell her father. A Cuban!"

In fact, the people were increasingly watching television.

The daily average viewing time per American household, as reported by the Associated Press, was four hours and thirty-five minutes in 1950; five hours and six minutes in 1960; five hours and twenty-nine minutes in 1965; five hours and fifty-six minutes in 1970; six hours and seven minutes in 1975.

News, sports and prime-time dramas were one thing. In 1969 there were thirteen soap operas on national television between the afternoon hours of twelve-thirty and four-thirty. According to network spokespeople at the time, eighteen million Americans watched soap operas daily, including six million men.

"What does all this mean?"
"I don't know. Call Professor Stokes."

The thirteen soap operas developed approximately two hundred and fifty million dollars in advertising revenues for the three networks a year.

Hot and cold water washes were in a death struggle. Besides oven cleaners, tub cleaners, toothpastes, burp pills and all the other high-priced substitutes for baking soda, there were advertisements for a foot soap which "makes your feet feel young again," a product which "works fast on any itch problem," bile salts, and a "fabric softener for your nose." (Before looking into afternoon television, I hadn't known a soft nose was a mark of beauty.)

"I don't like the idea of being careful when I kiss my wife!"

The production qualities of the commercials were vastly superior to the dramas that separated them by a very few minutes. Clearly the commercials, not the dramas between them, were the raison d'être of afternoon television.

It was the dramas, the stories, the soap operas themselves the people thought they were watching.

What these dramas said, and how they said it, to keep the people watching the commercials, remains an underrated gauge of a people at a time and place.

The elements making up the soap operas in 1969 were: violence, ill health (including social diseases), blackmail, bribery, unwed pregnancy, abortion, extramarital affairs, embezzlement, nymphomaniacy, incest (*Days of Our Lives* had a character suffer amnesia, from a first-degree burn yet, and fall in love with his sister—how forgetful can you get?), murder and drugs. By then, most of the soap operas had had an LSD incident. (On one program, a girl freaked out on the drug LSD for days, murdered somebody, then decided not to marry, as her child would be deformed).

Not ever mentioned, declared taboo by the networks, were the contraceptive pill (maybe you can see why), homosexuality, and religion (although they were not above identifying a character as Catholic).

And not ever mentioned, if you can believe it, was the war in Vietnam.

Tentative efforts, on *Love of Life* and *One Life to Live*, to integrate

black people into the plots brought sacks of complaining mail from
the viewers.

"We like to think we're civilized people living in a civilized society," said a network spokesperson. "But, like it or not, there are
certain moral codes."

Obladi, oblada, life goes on, bra!

A cultured man backed his conversation (through a pipe) with
good music from a record player. He wore a jacket and tie at all times,
even at home, and never left his bed for a glass of water or to investigate the gunshot in the next room without his robe.

An uncouth chap, on the other hand, showed a shank of leg
between sock and trouser cuff and wore sweaters or stripped to his
shirt at home.

Clearly, respectability was in having executive length hose, lapels
at all times. And, of course, in not being Cuban.

Villains, including out-of-towners, were always referred to by their
last names.

Regardless of the length of their socks, however, both the couth
and the un- had the same insatiable interest in other people's pregnancies, abortions, marriages and divorces. Although the bad fellow
used "ain't," both the blackmailer and the doctor apologized in the
same way for persistently bringing something up.

Whatever the profession (doctors and lawyers were at the top of
the social and goodness scale; doctors were nearly sanctified—on the
Soaps, at least, they still made house calls; acknowledgment of the
arts were characterized by only a few bearded architects) no one
seemed to get any work done. Men stood around in their sack suits,
women in their coifs ready to chew over any bit of dirt.

None of the nasty things referred to ever really happened on these
programs. They were only talked about.

It seemed that about forty percent of every conversation was spent
commenting on the conversation: *I would like to talk to you. Could I
talk to you for just a second? I have something I want to say to you. Go on,*

Dad. This is incredible. Well, truth is stranger than fiction. Don't you believe me? It's very difficult for me to go on with this story . . . (until you get that *#&% cue card over here) . . . I'm sorry, I didn't mean to pry. What do you expect me to say? I'm not sure you're understanding this. It's strange what the mind decides to retain. I ain't gonna say no more. No more'n I already have. May I ask you a question?

Obladi, oblada.

Despite all this fantastic gargling, the only device discernible in the Soaps was the "Flow of the Secret." A bit of scandal starts Here and you're supposed to hold your breath until it works through twenty characters to There. *Don't let Sandy tell Phil what Paul told Alice because if Sally finds out and tells Peter about Madge, what will Bob say to Fran?* Halfway through this process, another secret is started.

The ages of the characters were fantastic to contemplate. Although there may have been an occasional picturesque old person or child (*Search for Tomorrow* had a little boy, about seven, who would walk through every few weeks) by and large, grandmothers were fifty years old and grandchildren twenty. Which is pretty remarkable when young couples (those who lived in apartments) were in their mid-thirties and established couples (those who lived in houses) were in their mid-forties.

As far as the Soaps were concerned, contraceptive devices had not been invented yet, but they sure had something tricky going.

Little kids as little kids did not exist in the world of the Soaps. What happened to all those preggie ladies when it got to be napper and runny nose time was never reported.

Hitting the age of Social Security also made people disappear somehow down the Madison Avenue hopper.

"My good friend . . . we were in reformatory together."

When Dad got home from the office, the clock on the mantel said precisely five o'clock. Ten minutes later, the clock still said five o'clock.

Soap operas reported the events of only one or two days a week, the year 'round. (A thunderstorm on *Dark Shadows* lasted four days;

six, including the weekend). There were probably less than thirty *Days of Our Lives* in a year.

BUT THEY NEVER MISSED A HOLIDAY!

For some reason, although drinking was fairly continuous on afternoon TV, the only drink ever identified was brandy. That brandy should be *the* drink, for casual conviviality as well as for dinner and lunch was most curious. Americans drink so little brandy it doesn't even show up on consumers charts.

Do you suppose that someone decided that because brandy has, unjustifiably, a medicinal reputation, the viewers in the boondocks would think it more respectable?

"I'm absolutely delirious . . . it has nothing to do with being sober."

Going out to dinner was still the most fun. Although all the characters looked rosy-cheeked and healthy, including the character who was about to have a heart transplant, there was never a scene shot outdoors. People went to the theater, but never to the movies.

When the telephone rang, it was looked at with shock and foreboding, as if it were just invented and the characters were perplexed as to what to do with it. The longer distance the call, the longer people held the receiver in their hands after the conversation was over, marveling either at the finished communication, or the instrument itself.

A knock at the door always roused a guess as to who was there, which was always wrong. It was never Peter, to pass on the secret; it was always Alice, who didn't know the secret yet.

And the most significant thing, in all this most deceitful literature ever to gain such a wide audience, was that there was *never* a television on the set, even in the background, either on or off.

> *"Innocence and decency will prevail."*
> *"Will they?"*
> *"Well, at least they'll hold their own."*
> *Obladi, oblada, life goes on, bra!*

24 L. Francis Herreshoff

My work has no future at all. I know that. A few years.
—Andy Warhol

✦ ✦ ✦

It was the craftsmanship, you see, the lifelong devotion to how things, yachts, furniture, cars, anything that works, ought to be shaped, joined, put together to have any real permanence.

He lived in a great baronial stone pile, a "castle," the neighbors called it, overlooking Marblehead Harbor, a real to-hell-with-the-middle-class house and his neighbors felt he said to hell with them, the Marblehead middle class, each time he purred down Front Street erect behind his flowing white moustache, goatee, in his 1964 Ferrari, and indeed he did say to hell with them.

"Almost all the people today who have any money in this country have been here only a generation or two and have little education, little taste, little sense of beauty," he said.

And he would look at the ticky-tacky, tail-finned, plastic-hulled, aluminum-masted, styrofoam-buoyed, proudly owned yachts rubbing against each other in the harbor, and he would say, "To me they look just like floating swill," and he meant it, this last of all real yacht, great yacht designers.

But the neighbors also knew that their kids, the little ones, regularly stormed the castle and ran up and down his stairs and jumped up and down on his bed and watched him working for hours at his four lathes in the workroom on the top floor. L. Francis never sent them away.

The bronze sign on the wrought iron gate read L. Francis Herreshoff, Yachts, and if you went in the lower door after a rain you had to jump over a puddle on the stone floor. The rooms were shaped in a way people had long since forgotten how to shape rooms, with stucco walls, pointed doors, arches, low, short hallways, everything designed, arranged for functions people had also forgotten. He had bought the house in 1945 when the white-elephant market was particularly low. The main hall was a terrific jumble of furniture, antiques he had restored, furniture, beautiful stuff he had designed and built from scratch himself, not arranged for either use or display, but jammed together in city blocks of furniture on ancient oriental rugs. "Things drip here when there's a rain." Over the great, walk-in fireplace were Peale's matching, full-length portraits of Martha and George Washington, done at a younger age than anyone who has passed fourth grade ever thought Martha and George Washington were, given to great-grandfather John Brown, the wealthiest man in New England, by George Washington in gratitude for having picked up the tab for a large share of the American Revolution.

L. Francis was a bachelor, at seventy-six. "Never married. Been too damn busy." The lady who had been his secretary for about forty years had retired from him in flagging health. He was down to part-time housekeeping, part-time secretarial help.

So the house was pretty quiet. A lot of clocks he had restored ticked and he would look startled at you when a hunk of plaster crashed to the floor, wondering if you heard it, knew what it was. The one phone would ring and he would run down the three flights from the workroom to answer it, shouting into it 1920 style, answering a hundred technical questions on sail area, prow speed, draft, beam of any of the one hundred and ten yachts he had designed, ("I didn't go into business until I was thirty-six, thirty-eight, something like that") page and illustration questions on any one of the six books he had written (*An Introduction to Yachting*, 1963, Sheridan House, fifteen dollars, was rapidly moving closer to the *Bluejacket's Manual*, on store shelves) plus questions on any number of other things he had created and patented, from a pocket picture frame then being manufactured in Germany to a hoseless bilge pump which could also be used as a fire extinguisher.

"Every few days I get a call, a letter, asking for one of my designs," he said. His *Mobjack*, a forty-five-foot ketch design, had been built more than one hundred and fifty times. The *Golden Ball*, an awfully likable two-foot-draft, centerboard, forty-six feet, six inches over all, eleven-foot-beam ketch he designed in 1958 was being built three times when we talked. Naturally he received a commission each time a design of his was used. "Because of my bad disposition I guess my boats aren't too popular around here. But an awful lot are still built in England and Australia."

Sitting before his baronial fireplace in a straight, baronial chair, one leg slung over the chair arm, red flannel shirt, red plaid tie under his goatee, his imperial, he pooh-poohed all the stories about his family, sea stories actually, about their inevitable blindness, their foreign intrigue, their aloofness, shrewdly asking me to direct the reader's attention to his own book, *Captain Nat*, which was one hundred percent accurate, at the same time intriguing me, by denigration, with some stories I had never heard or had never really I-heard-heard.

"The first Herreshoff, Charles Frederick, came to this country in 1775, a Prussian. He had been brought up, educated in the court of Frederick the Great. Possibly he was Frederick's bastard son. I don't think he was. He didn't own anything. That's why it's remarkable he married John Brown's daughter. They fell in love with each other somehow or other."

"Does this mean you're a direct descendent of Frederick the Great?"

"It would. But it doesn't."

Possibly . . .

"My grandfather had three boats built for himself, which he had designed."

Herreshoff had already expressed irritation at the yacht *Yankee*, a publicized, European-built, world-cruise schooner. "It's a family name. The first *Yankee* was a privateer put out to sea by my family during the War of 1812." In 1924 he designed a famous yacht with a twenty-five-foot waterline called the *Yankee*.

"When my father, Nat Herreshoff (1848–1938), was a young man there weren't any yacht designers in this country, just modelers and boat builders. He was the first real designer in this country." Possibly one of the two or three greatest yacht designers there ever was or will be, anywhere. The *Reliance*, according to L. Francis Herreshoff, was perhaps his father's greatest, most important design, and surely one of history's most graceful ways of going to sea. The "New York Fifty" design, of which twelve were built in 1913, was our great common denominator. L. Francis Herreshoff had skippered one of them, the yacht *Barbara*, for a teenage summer, and so had I.

"They all had glaucoma—three uncles and one aunt—attacking them between the ages of fourteen and seventeen. I have it myself, but I take drops four times a day." He had already denied that his father, Nat Herreshoff, ever suffered one day of blindness, even in advanced age. "My father had the most remarkable eyes—he had Eye—of any man I've ever met." Despite the four drops a day and the glasses, the eyes of L. Francis, and the Eye, seemed remarkably precise: quick eye measurements I watched him take in his workroom were beyond mortal, this mortal's, comprehension.

"My Uncle John Herreshoff went blind as a boy, while he was building a fourteen-foot boat. My grandfather, whom you would now call a man of leisure, only there aren't any since taxes, insisted he finish the boat, helped him with it. This grew into a yacht-building yard within sight of the Herreshoff house in Bristol, Rhode Island, which John spent his life running. After a while, my father, Nat Herreshoff, went into partnership with him."

L. Francis was born in that same house. Each summer the family would move a mile to their estate. He described the playrooms of their houses being crammed with steam engines, boilers, hulls, for the boys to "fiddle with." His three older brothers were all educated to run the yacht business, and they did so to the extent of their personalities.

"I was educated as a farmer, sent to agricultural school. The plan was for me, the fourth son, to take over the estate. In those days fathers made decisions like that and no one ever questioned them. But I had skippered the yacht *Barbara* and that got me a commission in the navy in World War I, and after that I worked for Burgess for seven years."

Nat Herreshoff sold the yacht yard in 1925, to Haffenreffer. "Very wise of him," L. Francis said. "Herreshoff stock was at its highest then." In 1926, L. Francis Herreshoff moved to Marblehead and went into business for himself.

"I'm the only man in the world, still living, who has designed any of the bigger racing boats: Class M boats and J boats." An M Class has about twice the sail area of a twelve meter. "This has been so for about fifteen years now."

He mentioned as an aside that prior to World War I he had designed and built his own car.

"I had six or eight men working for me in 1935, but I discovered they were making more money than I was. I got rid of them. I've done all my own drawings since 1938."

We spoke of his famous boats, the *Landfall*, the *Istalena*, the *Yankee*. The one he mentioned most was the seventy-two foot *Ticonderoga*, which he designed in 1935 and which won the SKAW Race in 1966 (a triangular race off Denmark, Sweden and Norway) and which had the highest speed/length ratio of any sailboat ever built (between known places, timed by a third party). In the Pacific, the *Ticonderoga* sailed over two hundred and forty miles a day for eight successive days, averaging 10.2 knots, one knot faster than the twelve meter boats have ever been timed. (The yacht speed record was set in 1905 by the *Atlantic*, for averaging 14.2 knots for twenty-four hours. But she was one hundred and eighty-seven feet long).

In his workroom upstairs he developed his inventions, designs, made by hand little bronze saluting cannons which sold for two hundred and fifty dollars each, bronze gaff goosenecks, boomnecks, mast signal staffs, etc. for various boats of his design, upon orders from their owners. He had just finished a marvelous, fancy-grained, white oak table chest, beautifully hand done, with dovetailed joints, cleverly clasped, to the specifications of a woman in New York.

"I don't know what she wants it for."

On his designing board he had hand lettered the following:

> Let's call it the Republic again.
> Let's have law and order again.
> Let's have God-fearing judges again.
> Let's say the Lord's prayer again.

Only the last line said *Loard's* prayer because he was a lousy speller, he said, and anyway, he expected to have to do it again.

"For years my clients have been sending me tracts. I'm going to have this shrunk to send back to them. My tract."

I asked him which of the younger designers he liked.

"At the present time there isn't one designer in the whole world that's any goddamned good. No one knows how to draw. No one has any decency."

Decency? We talked then, of boats, yachts, of bronze and wood, of lettering by hand, of law and order, of dogs we knew and families, cars we'd like to know, of Godfearing judges and of the Republic, of the expectation of doing things again, of always doing things again until they are right, the way they ought to be, to be any good, to have any permanence, decency, *to be of any use.*

25 The American Dream, Rolling in Bread

"It's not supposed to happen," said blues singer Johnny Winter.

It was late at night. We were standing next to a floor-to-ceiling penthouse window looking out and down at the lights of the city. A small party was going on in the lit room behind us.

A performer, then unknown to us, named Roberta Flack had just played the piano and sung to us, astounding at least this observer.

And an impresario present had just given his instant opinion that Roberta Flack would never be able to work successfully before a large crowd.

I had withdrawn to the side of the party.

"Have all your dreams come true," Johnny Winter said, "become a success."

Only one of us reflected in the window. Being albino, only the reflection of Johnny Winter's dark shirt could be seen.

"But it has happened."

Johnny began digging the blues in the cotton fields of his Daddy's flop farm in Leland, Mississippi.

And he began singing the blues on the sidewalk outside a Chicago music store.

A December, 1968, article in Rolling Stone resulted in a six hundred thousand-dollar recording contract for Johnny with Columbia Records.

And for Columbia Records, instantly a million-dollar record called, Johnny Winter.

"I keep havin' the nightmare people are goin' to come and say, 'You

can't sing the blues no more, boy. You gotta go back. Sing rock. Sing soul.' I shudder."

It was weird, seeing my reflection in the window and not his.

"But it's not goin' to happen now. Not ever. It just can't."

◆ ◆ ◆

One hundred barefooted youngbodies, kids, some in their twenties, came into the room and saw a ton of month-old bread, some still in wrappings saying, Fresh Thursday, a pile three feet high, fifty feet in diameter. All this bread on the floor was there for us to play with. A clarinet-dominated band screeched through amplifiers from the stage. And there was as much of a light show as the rock club could muster on a bright Sunday afternoon.

John Fisher's Bread Happening.

The bread was snow and sand, to jump in, roll in, toss each other in, grab handsful of and fling at each other.

No throwing bread at the band, please.

Some kids were formally athletic, doing rolls in the bread. One hit beautiful two-baggers into the balcony, using buns and a breadstick.

Walking across the bread barefoot was like snowshoeing on a cloud. The band was playing "The Campbells Are Coming" in the galumphing fashion proper for that song.

I got hit on the nose with a bagel, then knocked over.

I sank into bread.

It was snowing whole wheat.

I was being beaten by crumbs. Bread was in my mouth, nose, ear, shirt, jeans.

I had always wanted to hit someone, anyone over the head with a bag of bread but, being well bred, I had never done so. Wot fun! It bursts beautifully over a person's head, pieces tumbling from head to shoulders, some flipping wide at the ears.

Some kids were creative. They drew to the side and made bread sculptures. One was of "The Beautiful Hollywood Star" with a hard-roll belly. Another did calligraphy in crumbs: "Better bread than dead." And another did a complicated bread painting he insisted was called *Summer Comes to Sherwood Forest.*

Still another tore out the middle of a piece of bread, leaving only the crust. He put this on a paper plate. Under it he wrote the title, comment, demand: More.

And some kids, of course, just sat in the bread and ate it.

To be honest, after a while the bread began to smell like the world after a good weep.

26 Louise Nevelson

A key myth of America is the solo figure with a guitar. It's the true American form, the singing cowboy. It will go on as long as the country will.

—Phil Ochs

✦ ✦ ✦

Louise Nevelson's house was on the corner of Spring and Mott streets in Greenwich Village, had seventeen rooms, and had been a private sanitorium.

After her assistant, Diana MacKown let you in through the red iron-grill door, and after you leapt over Diana's lemon-yellow bike in the tile foyer, you climbed up and up through the smell of cat and Chinese lacquer. It didn't seem to matter where you stopped. The walls were painted magenta and pale yellow and black and all the huge rooms and corridors were studios (works-in-progress and precious pieces seethed at you from all directions) only on some floor there was some sort of a center of consciousness, a bathroom with relentless plumbing and a kitchen out of which Diana promised you coffee.

We were all to talk in a room next to it around a long, hard table, sitting on hard, backless benches, suspended, as it were, in her work, the bubbling toilet being the only connection, it seemed, to the great stream of reality, the Out There.

"She may be the most eccentric lady in the arts," Remains Nameless had said. "Louise Nevelson is probably the top sculptress in the

211

country at the moment, but there's no knowing what she'll do, or say."

"I'd be delighted to see you," she said on the phone. Which was pretty eccentric.

Although she was about as old as the century, it wasn't until the "Ancient Games and Ancient Places" exhibit at the Grand Central Moderns in 1955 that Louise Nevelson began to emerge as a successful artist, by which people mean she began to sell. After her divorce, "I can't really remember: about 1930; I waited until Mike was about nine," she starved as a student under Hans Hoffman in Germany, again in New York the next year, starved as a mural-painting assistant to Diego Rivera (she starved with almost everybody worth starving with), the Works Progress Administration for much of the 1930s, Relief in the 1940s. At the time I met her, she was complaining that everybody was forgetting to mention a three thousand–dollar sculpture prize she had recently won in Brazil. Everybody was too busy mentioning the wall she had just done for the Detroit Museum, for which she grossed fifty-five thousand dollars. And her book, don't forget her book, *Homage to Edith Sitwell* (1967, Harry Abrams, Inc., one thousand dollars a copy; meant to be a gift item, I guess). Besides earrings and pins, which she also made (earrings, seventeen hundred dollars; gold and wood pins, three thousand dollars, available, as was her other work, through the Pace Gallery in New York), Nevelson estimated she had grossed a half a million dollars in the last ten years. "Certainly I'm a great seller. Now." In just twelve years she had gone from rags to earrings.

What she would do, by "recomposing the environment," was drop you in her setting as she would an egg to be poached. Uneven, fragmented black walls curved at you like the bubbling sides of a pan, isolated pieces, rough, sharp, black wood stood in some mysterious relation to each other around you; black, white, sharp bulks dangle from the ceiling. Superego, ego, id; shell, white, yolk: something happens. Black, white objects, mirror-backed spaces boil around you.

Needless to say, she had to enter the room from behind you, whichever direction you were facing.

She was wearing a green silk, apparently padded, babushka and a sort of droopy, apparently quilted, satin suit, on the hottest day of the year in Greenwich Village. Despite all her starving, it was clear her complexion had never been too many blocks from Helena Rubinstein's. She had on eyelashes with which you could paint a wall, which were so long you couldn't avoid painting a wall.

She was smoking a Tiparillo. She did not offer me one.

We sat at the table across from each other.

"The thing is, you see, I never questioned my ability. I starved. You know that. People, even cultured people, say they have to eat. I don't know why they have to eat, if they can't do what they want. I could never question myself.

"I believe in genes. I believe one is born with it. It was clear when I was four, five. All through school I automatically won the prizes."

Diana brought me coffee. She was visibly hot in a miniskirt. She confided in me later Nevelson thought air-conditioners unnatural.

"In those days, schools were different, you know," she went on, coffeeless and coolly. "They loved the child. From first grade through senior year I never had less than A. That gave me quite a sense of confidence, do you understand?"

I said I did, academically.

Her family moved from Kiev, Russia, in 1905, when she was four and a half, to Rockland, Maine. In Russia the Berliawsky family were in the lumber and real estate business, and they had been since, in Maine. A brother, Nathan, owned the Thorndike Hotel in Rockland.

"Some of us, there is something about us, that draws things out. As a child, I was too shy, too tall, too foreign. But I was chosen for everything, the basketball team, the choir, all the prizes. It's a contradiction. Everything is in reverse. If you make people understand the irony of a terribly shy person who is absolutely sure of herself, you'll make them understand me."

She was married in 1920 to Charles Nevelson, who was a partner in the Polish-American Navigation Company which, at that time, was an important shipping firm. Her only son, Michael, a sculptor, lived in Fairfield, Connecticut.

"I believe many people, perhaps the majority of people have talent. But I think it is covered by bad education, bad conventions. So few have the courage to break their way through. It would have been impossible for me to be stifled. I would have burned everything down."

During the years she was married to Nevelson, she took lessons in practically everything, drama, singing, speech, the dance.

"I had to, I was so terribly shy. I had to bring myself out."

She lit another Tiparillo. She did not offer me one.

"Life and art are inseparable for me. Life is art. It is a way of seeing things. It is the perspective that is important. Do you understand?"

"Yes."

"Christ, when told His mother was nearby, said, 'Who is my mother?' He had a job to do. That's the way I feel about my art, I must feel about my art."

Two little blonde sprites in pink shorts and jerseys bounced into the room: Elizabeth and Ree-ree.

"Hi, Grandma."

"Hi. Listen. We have new kittens." Grandma carefully held her cigar up while she kissed them. "Go see the kittens. This afternoon we'll go to Coney Island and then up to your father's lake."

"Great. Where's Nieth?"

Nieth was the eldest granddaughter.

"She's upstairs. In the tub."

They went off to find the kittens. One of them was in my lap, under the table.

"Men, you know, were caught up in a superficial concept of refinement. It was deadly. They believed in manners. In art, they believed in decoration. But I love the idea of taking the commonplace and exalting it. Today, people are developing a more structured, internal refinement. They go by feelings."

Originally, Nevelson became famous for her box sculpture. Ten years before she had popularized the sculpture of found objects.

"There is no such thing as the ugly. There is only the wrong perspective."

Nieth appeared in the doorway, looking hot and sleepy.

"Grandma. I can't take a tub."

"Why not?"

"The tub is full of kittens."

"Oh, well. They'll only be there a minute."

Nieth withdrew.

"Here's what I think. I don't say I make sculpture or paintings. It's embarrassing to say you make things. The search is for greater awareness, consciousness. My native feeling is and always has been—and it is native, nothing I intellectualized—I want everything around me to harmonize. I put things together, everything, objects and space, until they harmonize."

She was involved in the total design of a building, somewhere. It was a secret which building, where, as it was being built with public funds, or so I gathered, and she was without an architect's credentials. Never did hear how it came out.

"I am with what are called the beats and the hippies. Not long ago, industry took the best brains from the schools, for a price, and made of them puppets, slaves, controlled where they lived, and how they lived. Even the wives: they had to go to cocktail parties; they had to have one drink; they could not have three. The hippies are right. They see through this phoniness, this deprivation of personality. And I really believe their arts are healthier, more creative than any of the refined, decorative arts, which were deadly."

We then prowled around each other, in space, restrained only, I suppose, by the reality of the bubbling toilet. I went over the concepts she had listed, harmony, an expanding consciousness, a center of conviction.

She was on her third cigarillo.

"There is something in us, a center, which I want to tap," she said. "If you strip away all the pseudo things, the phoniness, you can move with the spirit."

"The only thing close to your philosophy I know of is the Navajo concept of *hozoji*."

"How can that be?" Her paint-brush eyelashes went up and down enough to do a whole wall. "I've never been associated with Indians."

"You must have been, somewhere, sometime. Keeping your environment in harmony by shifting your perspective so that you are free to move with the spirit is a Navajo belief. It is what made them great."

"The only thing I know about that," she said, "was Oliver LaFarge, who wrote *Laughing Boy*. We were great friends. We used to get drunk together at the 21, regularly. He was very interested in the Navajos, and I daresay I picked up some things from him. I guess we used to talk to each other an awful lot."

She continued, more slowly. "I had to get rid of my collection of Navajo pottery recently, about thirty pieces. I felt it was time it should go to a museum. I'm having someone in Ohio look around for me. No one knew I had it."

And most slowly, she said, "Any people whose abilities to design were that advanced must have been a most advanced civilization. Don't you think?"

"You mean, spiritually?"

"Yes."

"Yes. I do."

Late-twentieth-century sculpture was being at least partly influenced, through Louise Nevelson, by an early-twentieth-century writer who became famous, and rich I guess, by idealizing the Noble Savage, the Navajo. And what do you think of that?

27   Yippie

"I'll bet you're sick to death of these demonstrations."

"I am not." There had been one the day before, and the police-man, sixty, with a paunch, had been busy in it, controlling traffic, the pedestrians, the gawkers, the demonstrators, the counterdemn-strators. "I wish there were more of them. Got to shake these guys up in Washington somehow."

❖ ❖ ❖

Irrelevant eats peanuts. It has a vacuum cleaner at one end, and very little responsibility at the other.

—Comedian Jimmy Durante, responding to the Students for a Democratic Society, which termed many previously held American values "irrelevant."

❖ ❖ ❖

Just as the Duke of Orleans drew the people to Versailles to protest the lack of bread but really meant them to bring Louis XVI and Marie Antoinette into Paris as captives, the Yippie Life Festival to take place in Chicago during the 1968 Democratic National Convention, "the death festival," was promoted to the people as a jolly outing, but the organizers' intention was far more profound.

In April of 1968 I talked with the leaders of the Youth International Party, the scenarists, directors, promoters, stage managers of what was to happen in the streets of Chicago outside Convention Hall while "the whole world was watching": Abbie Hoffman, Jerry Rubin, Paul Krassner and the most articulate of all, Marty Carey.

What people say after an event they have planned is seldom as revealing as what they say while they are planning the event. And this was an event, probably the prime event of the era.

Early in 1968, the Youth International Party opened a public relations office on the sixth floor of 32 Union Square, New York City. When you dialed the number of the Youth International Party, the phone would be answered with "Yippie!"

The walls of the one-room office were festooned with happy signs advocating Life, Courage and Consciousness. When I first penetrated the office (in my favorite disguise as a Central Intelligence agent disguised as a newspaper reporter), seven kids were working like Santa's helpers, typing, licking envelopes, answering phones. The young girls, at sixteen, looked grandmotherly in amusing squarelensed glasses and the old girls, at twenty-two, looked preschool in miniskirts. The boys looked like they had just ridden nags from Nashville. At that moment they were sending out twenty thousand fliers advertising the Easter Yip-Out at Central Park. The office also endlessly put out what could only be described as advertising specialties: Yippie buttons, Yippie balloons, stove-pipe Lincolnesque hats which said "Yippie," posters, banners. Slogans include: We Demand the Politics of Ecstasy! and Rise Up and Abandon the Creeping Meatball!

"This is a much cheerier place to work than in a real political headquarters," said office coordinator Gloria Rutstein, who was twenty-one. "There isn't that same grim photo of a dying soldier on the wall."

Miss Rutstein had disturbed the establishment three years before by sending a letter to General Hershey, head of Selective Service, saying that under no circumstances would she register for the draft on her eighteenth birthday and signing the letter "G. Rutstein." For a period of months, she said, the Federal Bureau of Investigation kept her family's house under surveillance, waiting for the "G. Rutstein" they believed to be an unregistered eighteen-year-old male to emerge.

"Are you coming to our Life Festival in Chicago?" a sixteen-year-old girl asked me.

"How would I get there?"

"Come with me."

"How are you going to get there?"

"I don't know. But I'm going."

According to Rutstein, expenses of YIP's public relations efforts were expunged by a three-day YIP benefit at the Electric Circus, the vast blue nightclub in New York's East Village.

Gradually through that spring of 1968—the Youth International Party attracted a playful following.

At the first bloom of spring in San Francisco's Golden Gate Park, nearly one hundred kids had a Strip-In. They took off all their clothes and sat down on the grass together. It was reported that the Fuzz thought they were too slippery to arrest that way, and no one got pinched.

Later in March there was a Yip-In one afternoon in New York's Grand Central Station, advertised by handbills as "a spring mating service celebrating the equinox, a back-scratching party, a roller-skating rink, a theater, with you as performer and audience."

Six thousand young people in funny costumes crammed the station, released Yippie balloons to its celestial ceiling, and stood about smoking pot. When a few kids climbed to the roof of the information booth, an important symbol of America without which few 1940 movies could have been made, and tore the hands off the clocks, the Fuzz charged. Two uniformed policemen hurled *Village Voice* reporter Don McNeill through a glass door without opening it, causing a gash in his scalp that required five stitches. Sixty-one persons were arrested and twenty were taken to hospitals with other than self-inflicted wounds.

"People who come to Yippie demonstrations are very reasonable," Ed Sanders, poet and leading, kindly light of The Fugs, said later. "There was no reason to rush in and crunch."

The Yip-Out on the Sheep Meadow in New York's Central Park on Easter attracted twelve thousand people. Four fully amplified bands played. Incense and maryjane burned. A plane lazed back and forth across the sky, dropping twenty thousand flowers. One hundred rabbits were released. Columbia Records handed out five thousand records. The police stayed away until dark, when fifteen came to protect a fire truck which had bounded over the meadow to put out a fire the yippies had set to keep warm. For every fire put out, the yippies lit two. When there were enough fires, the police and fire truck went away, leaving the yippies to put out the fires themselves, as they had originally intended.

Yippies parodied an earlier well-publicized police raid at New York State University at Stony Brook, Long Island, by sneaking up on the campus at dawn, and then dashing through it shouting, "Boo! Boo!"—which is another word for marijuana.

They also invaded the Manhattan offices of Consolidated Edison in a Pollution Protest, presented secretaries with black chrysanthemums and blew soot they had brought in bags at the executives.

In May, YIP organized a National Indian Ghost Danee (originally choreographed by the Sioux in the late nineteenth century to bring back the buffalo) to make United States foreign policy disappear.

All this spring foolishness was reported faithfully by the media. "A name like yippie is a natural media manipulator," said Paul Krassner, editor of *Realist* magazine and, of course, YIP leader.

◆ ◆ ◆

The cradle of the Youth International Party, like the cradle of all great American entertainments, political parties, utopian dreams, riots and baseball games, was a candy store, in this case, Gem's Spa, on the corner of Second Avenue and St. Mark's Place, in New York's East Village. Unlike the more usual American loiterer, maintaining the same posture, costume and thought process standing outside the village candy store as he would covering shortstop, the yippie outside Gem's Spa looked shriveled inside his electric hairdo, mod clothes, and he told you that what he thought about most in those days was your giving him a dollar.

East Village, which that spring was really only one block of loiterers along St. Mark's Place, was about ten blocks northeast of Greenwich Village. Running between them was a tourists' artery, Eighth Street, of expensive junk shops and prosperous mod clothing stores. Walking into the East Village from the southwest you immediately saw its past and its present: a decrepit steam bath on your right, and on your left, an enormous electric blue building, which was the Electric Circus.

I was met, for our very secret meeting, at Gem's Spa and led deep into the bowels of some building on St. Mark's Place.

We sat cross-legged around the walls of a small room like Indians around a tribal fire. Ordinary cigarettes burned in an ashtray on a low coffee table in our center.

"You're sitting in the very spot the idea of the Youth International Party was conceived," Marty Carey said.

"Yippie."

A joint of "the last good stuff from Vietnam" was passed around the circle like a peace pipe, from left to right. In keeping with Indian tradition, perhaps unconsciously, whoever had the joint also seemed to have the automatic right to speak.

In the next room, a rock station had been turned up to almost total sound.

Marty Carey had already told me that their purpose in starting the Youth International Party was "to offer the people an alternative lifestyle. Something to do other than to conform or die."

Now he was saying, "We're the first generation that doesn't have to worry about material things. I know from my own experience I can live off the garbage of this civilization. I have this wonderful feeling of free time, not like my dad waiting all year for two weeks off."

Carey, who was thirty, sold his paintings for money. "We exchange garbage," he said, and when asked his background, said: "I was kicked out of Yale." In fact, he received his degree from Yale College in 1961, and was expelled from Yale graduate school for insisting the head of his department was a liar. He could have received his master's degree in fine arts from Ohio State if he could only have brought himself to type up his thesis.

He said, "My parents never interfered in anything I ever did."

"Everything I do is rebellion from what I was taught to do at home," said Jerry Rubin, a graduate of the University of Cincinnati. "Straight down the line. What my father thought of money, career, of time. It is impossible to live so compartmentally."

Rubin worked as a reporter for the *Cincinnati Post & Times-Star* for five years before coming to New York, where he wrote freelance for the underground press.

"The family structure is breaking down, has broken down," said Abbie Hoffman, who would not admit to being over thirty, but was. "The family is no longer a vertical structure, but a horizontal structure. Everybody of our generation is brother and sister."

Hoffman had worked for SNCC and the Stuart Hughes campaign for senator from Massachusetts.

Hoffman and Carey, both from Worcester, Massachusetts, had played high school football against each other. Asked how he supported himself, Hoffman answered: "I steal." (After *Woodstock Nation,* he was to publish a book, on his own, called *Steal This Book,* which few stores carried, for an obvious reason.)

"There's something weird about the family," Rubin said.

"For the Kennedys and that whole era there's the Frank Sinatras, the individuality. Today you've got the Beatle-type structure. You examine that closely, and you'll see everything," Hoffman said. "The whole booze era, Las Vegas, sin. The Frank Sinatra culture was solo. The Beatles are communal."

"For my parents there was the big-business model: the man. Today there is the group-communal model,"

Carey said. "Our models are the American Indians, the tribal image. Not the lonely American cowboy."

Carey said, "A whole bunch of people living together, having children, none of them married. Like that."

"I once got married to a whole bunch of people," Krassner said. "Over at radio station WBAI."

"And I got married to a whole lot of people the next day," Carey said.

"Is there a difference between LSD and chopped liver?" Hoffman asked the ceiling. "If there is, we're a new community."

Marty Carey was married in the conventional sense, and Paul Krassner had been until recently. They both had their children in private schools.

"For most people, money is the one thing that inhibits freedom," Rubin said. "How to get it and how to spend it. That's all they live for."

"In this society either all the money or none of it is freedom," Carey said. "Choose your fantasy."

"Burning the dollar bill is our supreme sacrifice for freedom," Carey said. "I mean our supreme demonstration."

Besides burning money, the Youth International Party advocated not only ending war, but abolishing all armies; free food; a heart transplant for President Lyndon Johnson; juvenile exhibitionism, *Take Kids Out of Clothes!*; legislation of psychedelic drugs; free public toilets.

I asked them the source of their wit. Rousseau hadn't been so funny.

"We're organizing six-year-olds," Carey said. "How can we be serious?"

It was then Paul Krassner uttered the wittiest line of the decade: "In terms of nature, God did not intend for there to be subways or Ed Sullivan." He continued: "If you have a cosmic point of view, you have a sense of absurdity. We see ourselves as absurd, too. Some come to this view of absurdity through drugs. It goes back to when you were a kid. You got attention by being a show-off.

"But what really brings it on is the awareness of death," he concluded. "The first time you become aware of death you see how transitory everything is. Nothing is serious."

Absurdity brought them to a discussion of politics.

"The whole political structure is irrelevant because it's not geared to chaos," Hoffman said. "Something astounding, happens, like Johnson's saying he was dropping out of politics and the whole media empire says Wha'? Um—Squak! Anything can happen and we'll survive. Chaos is what we are. We're used to switching from Vietnam to Jackie Gleason in a fraction of a second. And we have no aristocratic sense of what is good and bad taste. Everything's the same chaos."

"I'd like to turn on television and have them say, 'and now the President,'" Carey said, "and have a big, blank screen, an electric miasma, and have the thing blow up."

"By the way," Rubin said, "Phil Ochs wants to set up a meeting between Bobby Kennedy and ourselves. Jack Newfield can set it up. But I told him we'd meet with him only under certain conditions."

"Why does he want to meet with us?" Krassner asked.

"He doesn't want to meet with us. Phil Ochs wants us to meet with him."

Phil Ochs dropped out of the Youth International Party a few weeks after he helped originate it. (Phil Ochs's name was included in the *Royal Blue Book of London*, an international listing of people "of family." Jack Newfield wrote a column for the *Village Voice*.

"In three months we'll hear Kennedy use the phrase 'to develop a new community,'" Hoffman said. "'We must develop an alternative lifestyle,' he'll say."

"He doesn't know his reassessment from his elbow," Krassner said.

Rubin said: "Jack Kennedy was a lot more interesting."

Krassner said: "He used to take a phrase and reverse it."

"Bobby just repeats it," Rubin said.

"I don't think it matters who becomes president," Carey said. "It will just delay the action. Kids who want to drop out will pin their last hopes on Kennedy but they'll still drop out later when they run into the middle-class world. I wouldn't like Kennedy to win because it will just delay the inevitable."

Hoffman said, "The trouble with our system of government is that Kennedy regards youth as one more pressure group, like Negroes or labor."

Time magazine had estimated there might have been as few as four hundred "hardcore yippies" nationwide.

To which hardcore intelligence Ed Sanders had nodded solemnly and stated, "Yes, I figure there are about a quarter of a million of us."

Carey said, "Already you can drive across country and never leave your friends, from Boston to Berkeley. There are yippies who will put you up everywhere."

"Activity is the language of our generation," said Hoffman. "It's not possible to be passive today. For example, when you walk down the street with long hair and sit on a sidewalk you've got to be prepared to deal with the way people will react to you. Being different from the stereotype is basically being active. Just being is subversive."

"I've been thrown out of three restaurants in Washington for long hair," Rubin said.

"We ought to have a Hair-In," Krassner said.

"The funny thing is I was with black people, too."

"What we're trying to do is create a second society," Carey said. "This is why we call attention to ourselves and try to let people know about us. What we're trying to create is a liberated soul, free from the middle class, negative in reaction to it. We figure we get so many people together and we can do whatever we want, be free, with most of us safe."

Rubin said, "There will be three societies in this country: black, white, and drop out."

"The thing is that as far as our society is concerned, we have a choice," Krassner said. "In being white. Therefore our dropping out is more of a protest."

"The blacks are oppressed," Hoffman said. "We're alienated."

"Even television distortion helps," Krassner said. "Showing the freakiest people on television at a Yip-In for example, really helps. People viewing say, 'If someone can look that wild then I can look a little weirder, freer than I do and get away with it.'"

"It's a two-civilization thing mainly because of television," Hoffman said. "There have been no great books in the last eight years. Movies, poetry, painting, but no books."

Rubin said, "What do you mean? We're all waiting for your book."

"Well, ah . . . it's not in linear form."

"I don't know," Krassner said. "I was in an elevator the other day and it occurred to me I was glad the elevator inspector hadn't dropped out."

"There are self-service elevators," Hoffman said.

"Not self-service elevator inspectors."

I asked if run-ins with the police would dim their enthusiasm for taking on the mess Chicago was liable to become during the Democratic Convention.

"Whenever we create a life celebration in the free streets, there's a kind of paranoiac reaction. People don't want to believe there is this real freedom," Carey said. "But the more we're pressed together the more we become a community.

"Our style doesn't depend upon our making demands upon the society," Carey continued. "Which is why we make such unreal demands upon society, like burn money and abolish the army."

Rubin said, "It's the quality of our lives that makes a life alternative necessary. What the cities look like when you walk around the streets, you know?"

The following lines were delivered with conscious smirks. I, the media, was being manipulated.

"The National Life Festival was planned before the Democratic Convention was scheduled," said Hoffman. "We picked the dates in Chicago more than a year ago and then later heard that the Democrats picked the same dates for their convention."

"We thought it would be nice for everybody to meet for a Yip-In at the end of the summer," said Marty Carey, "after everybody had spent the summer looking for quiet pockets to take up residence, as far away, as isolated from the crowded middle-class urban society as possible. Chicago seemed the most central place."

So one nice Saturday, yippies Abbie Hoffman, Jerry Rubin, Paul Krassner and Bob Fass flew to Chicago to ask Mayor Daley for the use of Grant Park for a campground during that week. Reports of the interview were garbled. From what I understood, Abbie Hoffman approached the mayoral desk, extended a flower, and said, "I love you," and Mayor Daley muttered something or other about, "I was afraid something like this would happen," and everybody flew home again without the park.

"We'll use it anyway," announced the requited Hoffman. "It's a public park. . . ."

✦ ✦ ✦

The above report, broken in two sections, was published on subsequent Sundays in the spring of 1968.

When I met with the Youth International Party organizers on St. Mark's Place, President Lyndon Johnson had just announced he would not run again for president.

A few days after the first section of this piece was published, Senator Robert Kennedy, who was running for president, was assassinated.

And a few days after the second section of this piece was published, the apartment on St. Mark's Place where we met was raided by various police authorities. Arrests resulted.

What happened in the streets outside the Democratic National Convention in Chicago that summer is history. It's all on film.

Indeed, the whole world was watching.

28 The Absolute End

Normally, I don't do interviews, as they too frequently are just so much hyperbole, but when the studio representative called and mentioned *that name* I said I was on, even though it would mean considerable travel—at studio expense, of course.

"I want you to understand," the representative said, "that this is a well-deserved rest for her, at her hideaway ranch in the mountains above Aspen, Colorado, and you're the only one she'll see during this period."

I packed my American Tourister Air-Flite and Smith Corona Sky-Riter and left my Ford Thunderbird at the airport.

After shaving inflight aboard Trans World Airlines from Chicago with my Noxema Mentholated and Wilkinson Sword Blade, her own driver whose name, he said, was Tucci, escorted me to her Jaguar XKE.

"That's a 1,750-foot drop," Tucci said prophetically, pointing off to the right as the Jag climbed the mountainside.

I had been reading Harold Robbins's latest book, *The Betsy*.

"A very thin guardrail, Tucci," I noted over the rims of my Montgomery-Frost reading glasses.

At just that moment, the NBC *Today* show was on, and that made me wonder how my dear friend, Dick Cavett was doing.

Dressed in Lady Lindley jodhpurs and Barr-Better-Built Boots and a Kerr print blouse, she greeted me at the door of her Bill Wilson–designed hacienda with a live cobra snake draped over her shoulders.

"Don't worry," she said, smiling that wonderful, enigmatic smile. "Henri's been fixed."

Slipping the snake off her shoulders and handing it to her house-boy whose name, he said, was Pucci, she added: "Now don't you say anything nasty about us Hollywood women taking the sting out of all you snakes."

In her living room, decorated by Jason Sherwood with Fulbright Furnishings, she said, "Do sit down. You must be exhausted after your trip. We'll have Dom Perignon champagne before you change for drinks before lunch."

Settling on the divan and sipping the champagne which Pucci brought, she asked: "Are you one of those writers who put a lot of yourself in your stories? I do hope so. I'm sure you're a lot more interesting than I am.

"There's one thing I want to get perfectly straight." Her champagne glass was set firmly on the coffee table. "Henry Kissinger and I aren't even friends. I've never even met the man. And it is utterly untrue that I accompanied him on his most recent trip to China."

I showered and changed before lunch, using Brut cologne, and changed into my After-Six white flannels, open-throated Arrow flaming pink shirt and Saracen sandals.

We ate intimately under an umbrella by the pool after sips of Ron Bacardi Rum–Coca Colas which Pucci brought.

"I love John Huston," she said. "And Alfred Hitchcock. I'd do anything he asked. Antonioni's a dear, and Peter Bogdanovich, isn't he brilliant, and Norman Jewison and Bergman, of course, and Truffaut and Bernie Bertolucci, Buñuel, Chabrol, De Sica, Fellini, Godard, Georgie Hill, Kazan, Leger, Louis Malle, Sam Peckinpah, Jean Renoir, Johnny Schlesinger, Truffaut (did I say his name once? that's the way I feel about him), Roger Vadim, Michael Ritchie, Billy Wilder, Peter Yates and last but not least, Cesare Zavattini."

She uncrossed her white, flared, Living Theater slacks and said: "Now I must absolutely rush for my massage."

While napping, I read Billy Worthy's exciting new screenplay which, it is rumored, 20th Century has an op on.

Shaving before dinner, this time with a Gillette blade and Mennen's cream, I wondered if I shouldn't ring my old friend, Cary Grant, and tell him how excited I am to hear he's planning a film, *Death Chatter*, with my old pal, Clint Eastwood. For dinner I wore my Lord & Taylor gray slacks and the forest green jacket fashioned by Neiman-Marcus.

Drinks were martinis on the rocks made with Tanqueray Gin, Noilly Prat Vermouth and of course just a dash of Sunkist lemon. The rocks were frozen Perrier water.

"I've never had a good role in my life," she said, dipping into her lobster bisque, which Pucci had brought us.

"I turned down the lead in *Cabaret* because I just couldn't see myself doing the Marlene Dietrich bit, not again.

"And I turned down the stage lead for *Applause*. I mean, how could anybody honorable take on a title like that?

"And you know I turned down Tevye in *Fiddler on the Roof.* Women's liberation can be pushed just so far.

"At present, I'm being sought for a variety of exciting new roles."

The moon was on the left shoulder of a mountain as Tucci picked me up at the front door.

Driving down the mountain, we crashed through the guardrail and fell the 1,750 feet—an accident which neither of us, I'm sorry to report, survived.

Epilogue

The Education of Gregory Mcdonald

The population of our nation has about doubled since we were born. Have our sensibilities diminished?

Technology, applicable to matters most personal, our health and sexuality, to most public and universal information collection, storage, dispersal, thermonuclear weapons and utilities, has developed more during our lives than in all world history before our births.

Yet during our lives have occurred history's most atrocious anti-Semitic and racist events; sexism continues; wars based on religious, racial, territorial disputes abound; factual ignorance and starvation increase in accelerating proportion to the world population.

No matter who I am or what I do, whether I do my work well or ill, couch my life in smiles or frowns, these are the mind-splitting realities of my existence.

Reconciling differing realities is the job of any generation. Failure to attempt to do so, I am convinced, leads to personal and universal peril.

—Gregory Mcdonald

ABOUT THE AUTHOR

Twice the winner of the Edgar Allen Poe Award and described by critics as the inventor of the sunlight mystery and "the Master of the Pointed Story," GREGORY MCDONALD published twenty-six books, including the bestselling *Fletch* series. From 1966 to 1973 he wrote for the *Boston Globe*, where he was among the earliest independent voices in the major media against the Vietnam War. He died in September 2008.